Teen Rape

Teen Rape

Look for these and other books in the Lucent
Teen Issues series:

Teen Addiction
Teen Alcoholism
Teen Depression
Teen Drug Abuse
Teen Pregnancy
Teen Prostitution
Teen Runaways
Teen Sexuality
Teen Smoking
Teen Suicide
Teen Violence

Teen Rape

by Lynn Slaughter

TEEN ISSUES

LUCENT
BOOKS®

THOMSON
———＊———™
GALE

San Diego • Detroit • New York • San Francisco • Cleveland • New Haven, Conn. • Waterville, Maine • London • Munich

THOMSON
─────✦─────™
GALE

LIBRARY OF CONGRESS CATALOGING-IN-PUBLICATION DATA

Slaughter, Lynn, 1947-
  Teen issues : teen rape / by Lynn Slaughter.
    p. cm. — (Teen issues)
Includes bibliographical references and index.
  ISBN 1-56006-513-3
  1. Rape—Juvenile literature. 2. Acquaintance rape—Juvenile literature. [1. Rape.
2. Acquaintance rape. 3. Incest. 4. Sexual abuse victims.] I. Title: Teen rape. II. Title.
III. Series: Teen issues (San Diego, Calif.)
  HV6558.S56 2004
  362.883'0835—dc22
                                                                        2003026298

Printed in the United States of America

Contents

INTRODUCTION 8

CHAPTER ONE 10
Teenagers Are Especially Vulnerable to Rape

CHAPTER TWO 21
The Causes of Rape

CHAPTER THREE 34
Risk Factors for Rape

CHAPTER FOUR 47
The Impact of Rape

CHAPTER FIVE 57
Recovering from Rape

CHAPTER SIX 67
Intervention and Prevention

NOTES 83
ORGANIZATIONS TO CONTACT 89
FOR FURTHER READING 91
WORKS CONSULTED 93
INDEX 106
PICTURE CREDITS 111
ABOUT THE AUTHOR 112

Introduction

THROUGHOUT HISTORY, RAPE—forcible sexual intercourse without consent—has occurred in most cultures around the world. Usually understood as aggression against women, rape has also been used against slaves and prisoners and other social groups who traditionally lack power or status. During wars, widespread raping of women has also served as a means of humiliating, degrading, and demoralizing enemies. When anthropologist Peggy Reeves Sanday studied 156 tribal societies, dating from 1750 B.C. to the late 1960s, she found that rape was particularly common in male-dominated, violence-prone societies in which women had little or no political power.

In contemporary times, rape has continued to be a widespread global problem. In one recent example, soldiers on both sides of the Bosnian war between Croats and Muslims in the 1990s regularly committed gang rapes and forced women to act as prostitutes and sexual slaves. Researchers estimate that at least twenty thousand women were raped, most of whom were Muslims.

News of the Bosnian atrocities shocked and horrified Americans, most of whom felt far removed from such lawlessness. Americans have traditionally taken pride in living in a democracy, governed by the rule of law. Most citizens believe in the ideals of justice, fairness, and respect for the worth and dignity of every individual. They are strong advocates of human rights, including the right to be safe from violent sexual assault and degradation.

However, despite an encouraging decline in the overall incidence of rape from 1993 to 2002, rape remains a widespread and serious problem in the United States. According to the Rape, Abuse, and Incest National Network (RAINN), every six minutes a rape or attempted rape takes place somewhere in America. For sexual assault—a broader category that the U.S. Department of Justice uses to classify rape, attempted rape, and other violent felonies that fall short of rape—the estimated frequency is every two minutes. And the group at greatest risk for rape and sexual assault is teenagers, especially teenage girls.

Rape is a topic that makes many people of all ages uncomfortable. Few people think of themselves as potential rape victims, and even fewer consider themselves capable of the rape of another. The natural reluctance to talk about the issue and the widespread existence of mistaken ideas about rape have resulted in a great deal of secrecy, silence, and shame surrounding the subject.

Lack of understanding, awareness, and open communication about rape only adds to the suffering of victims. Since rape affects teenagers more than any other group in society, teens deserve and need accurate information about its causes and effects.

1

Teenagers Are Especially Vulnerable to Rape

SINCE THE EARLY 1970s, an explosion of research has revealed that teenagers are at special risk for rape. Study after study indicates that adolescents have the highest rates of rape victimization of any age group, and supports the conclusion of the National Victim Center and the Crime Victims Research and Treatment Center that rape is essentially "a tragedy of youth."[1] According to the U.S. Department of Justice's 1999 National Crime Victimization Survey, girls between the ages of sixteen and nineteen are raped or sexually assaulted at thirty-five times the rate of older women. The Justice Department's National Violence Against Women Survey found that more than half of female rape victims were younger than age eighteen when they experienced their first attempted or completed rape, and the FBI estimates that one in three girls is a victim of some form of sexual assault. Moreover, being raped as a child or adolescent puts young people at much greater risk for sexual assault as an adult. Women who were raped as minors are twice as likely to be raped as adults than women with no history of sexual assault.

While most rapists are male and most victims are female, males can be victims as well. The FBI estimates that one in six boys is a victim of sexual assault while growing up.

Rape: the "hidden crime"

Despite these statistics, no one knows for sure how many people experience rape. Experts often refer to rape as the "hidden crime" because most rapes are never reported. This is perhaps not surprising. While rape is never the victim's fault, victims often blame themselves and feel guilty and ashamed. Some are afraid of what will happen to them if they tell. Will others believe them? Will their family and friends blame them? Will their assailant come after them again? If they pursue legal action, will their character and credibility be attacked in the media and the courts, as has happened in some highly publicized cases?

Victims are especially reluctant to make a report if they know their assailant, which is usually the case. In a study by the National Center for the Prevention and Control of Rape, 92 percent of adolescent rape victims said they knew their attacker.

Concerned about the reactions of parents, friends, and their assailant(s), young people are the least likely of all to report being attacked. When sixteen-year-old Mary (throughout this book, names of individuals have been changed to protect their privacy) was raped by her boyfriend in a parking lot, the only person she told was her best friend, whom

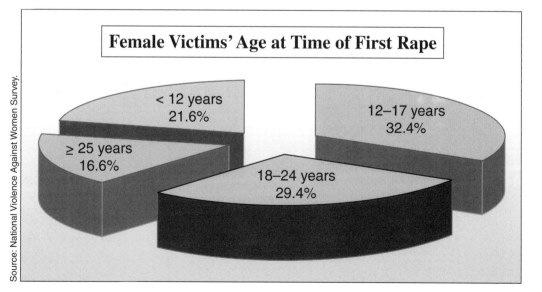

Female Victims' Age at Time of First Rape

< 12 years
21.6%

12–17 years
32.4%

≥ 25 years
16.6%

18–24 years
29.4%

Source: National Violence Against Women Survey.

she swore to secrecy: "No way was I going to tell my parents. It would have come out that we'd had sex before. They would have blamed me for what happened."[2]

Some teenagers do not tell because they are confused about whether what happened to them was really rape. Like many adults, when they think of rape, they think of a stranger lurking in the bushes, not someone they know and trust. Some of the confusion stems from the dramatic changes in recent years in how rape is defined.

The changing definition of rape

Prior to the 1960s, the legal definition of rape was the "carnal knowledge of a woman not one's wife by force or against her will."[3] In 1962, the definition in the newly established U.S. Model Penal Code was updated and made more explicit: "A man who has sexual intercourse with a female not his wife is guilty of rape if . . . he compels her to submit by force or threat of force or threat of imminent death, serious bodily injury, extreme pain, or kidnapping."[4]

This definition did not include any recognition that males could be raped or that a marriage partner could be raped by a spouse. It also did not include forced oral or anal intercourse. In the 1970s, armed with a growing body of research, activists in the reemerging women's movement successfully pressed for a broader legal definition of rape. Since then, extensive rape reform legislation has been enacted throughout the country.

The legal definition of rape has changed dramatically. The U.S. Department of Justice currently defines rape as vaginal, anal, or oral penetration by the offender(s) forced upon a male or female victim either through verbal threats or overt physical force. It includes incidents where the penetration is from a foreign object such as a bottle and recognizes that rape can be either a heterosexual or same-sex act.

According to current state and federal laws, rape also includes taking advantage of an incapacitated victim, who is unable to give consent. It is rape if an assailant penetrates a victim who is unconscious, under the influence of drugs or alcohol, or has a mental disability, physical disability, or illness.

Date rape

The vast majority of teen victims, both male and female, are raped by someone they know. The term for nonstranger rape is acquaintance rape. One of the most common types of acquaintance rape is date rape, in which the rapist is a dating partner. Since the peak dating years begin in adolescence, teens are especially vulnerable to date rape.

For example, Christa, a high school freshman, enjoyed making out with her boyfriend, a popular senior football

The majority of teen rape victims are raped by an acquaintance. Many are victims of date rape, in which the rapist is a dating partner.

player. She did not, however, feel ready to have intercourse with him. One night, they were making out in his van when he told her: "It's time to finish what you started."[5] He pinned her against the seat and raped her, even though she tried to push him away and begged him to stop.

Inexperienced in sexual encounters, teens like Christa are at special risk for rape and assault by a dating partner. In the Massachusetts Youth Risk Behavior Survey, a study of more than two thousand female high school students, one in five girls reported being "hit, slapped, shoved, or forced into sexual activity by dates."[6]

For some adolescents, particularly adolescent girls, rape is not a one-time event but part of an ongoing abusive dating relationship in which they are subjected to a combination of verbal, emotional, physical, and sexual abuse. In Barrie Levy's book, *Dating Violence,* Salina Stone describes the pattern of abuse by her teenage boyfriend: "He would beat me, then rape me. It was supposed to be a loving gesture to make up for when he beat me. That was when I started trying to break up with him. But he would come back crying, 'I love you, I'll never hurt you again.'"[7]

In an article on adolescent battered women, health writer Nancy Worcester reports that many adolescent women are beaten up if they try to insist that their boyfriends wear condoms or abstain from sexual activity. When the sexual violence in an abusive dating relationship results in pregnancy, the abuse often gets worse. "Because battering so often starts or accelerates during pregnancy and because sexual assault and other forms of violence are so intimately connected, anyone who works with adolescent pregnancy or sexual assault needs to be aware of the connections,"[8] says Worcester.

Gay and lesbian teens are also vulnerable to rape in abusive relationships. These teens are even less likely to tell anyone, for fear of the reactions of family and friends to their sexual orientation. Elizabeth, for example, became involved in a secret love affair with Cheryl when she was fifteen. Cheryl repeatedly punched her, put her down, threatened suicide, and forced her to have sex with her. When Elizabeth tried to break up with her, she recalls that Cheryl "stood out in the middle of the street and yelled at me, threatened to bring me 'out,' took my things or locked me out of my own house."[9]

Casual-acquaintance or friend rape

In some cases, an acquaintance rapist is not someone the victim is dating but rather someone he or she knows as a friend or casual acquaintance.

A widely publicized acquaintance-rape case took place in 1986 in a wealthy suburb of Connecticut. The attack occurred when sixteen-year-old Adrienne Bak asked eighteen-year-old Alex Kelly for a ride home from a party. She did not know him very well, but she could not imagine there would be any problem. Alex was a popular star on the local high school's wrestling team, he had a devoted girlfriend, and Adrienne and Alex had friends in common.

Instead of taking her home, however, Alex drove Adrienne to a dead-end street and parked in a secluded area. Then he pinned her body down with his leg, grabbed her throat, and raped her. "He said he was going to make love to me, and if I didn't let him, he'd kill me,"[10] Adrienne testified in court when the case finally came to trial a decade later.

Like Adrienne, many teenage victims are caught off guard by acquaintance rapists. They report being totally unprepared for an assault by someone they knew who seemed like a normal, friendly person. As Phyllis Harris, a community education coordinator for the Cleveland Rape Crisis Center, explains: "He's a classmate, a guy you're dating, your brother's friend—someone you've seen around and feel comfortable with. That's why it's so devastating—you are violated by someone you thought you could trust."[11]

A technological twist on acquaintance rape: danger on the internet

Many teens go online and spend time in chat rooms in search of advice, friendship, and sometimes romance. Inexperienced at relationships and, in general, less aware than adults of the importance of skepticism about online strangers, teenagers can become victims of Internet predators who pretend to be someone they are not.

For example, Steffi met a guy online who told her he was, like her, seventeen. They e-mailed for months. He seemed great, and Steffi could hardly wait to meet him in person. When they decided to get together, he told her to meet him at a local outdoor hangout. Steffi recalls: "He showed up and grabbed me, covered my mouth and dragged me behind a building. There were people around, but they just thought we were making out. This guy was an adult, and he handcuffed me, raped me and left me there. I woke up in the emergency room."[12]

A survey by *Family PC* magazine indicated that sexual predation and harassment on the Internet are proliferating. More than one-third of online teens say they have been approached in chat rooms with inappropriate sexual content. Teens often do not tell their parents because they are afraid of losing their online privileges.

Statutory rape

Even if Steffi had consented to sexual intercourse with her online adult acquaintance, he could have been arrested for statutory rape. Every state has a statutory-rape law that prohibits adults from having sexual intercourse with minors under the age of consent, which ranges from sixteen to eighteen. Statutory-rape laws assume that young people are unable to give meaningful consent to sexual activity with adults, particularly in cases where adults are in positions of authority over them, such as teachers or bosses. A highly publicized statutory-rape investigation involved the late Michael Kennedy, a member of the prominent Kennedy family. In 1997, he was accused of engaging in an affair with the teenage baby-sitter of his three children. The case was later dropped when the young woman refused to cooperate with investigators.

In recent years, there has been a renewed interest in vigorously enforcing and strengthening statutory-rape laws because of research indicating that a significant number of minor girls are impregnated by their adult boyfriends.

According to David Landry and Jacqueline Darroch Forrest, researchers with the New York–based Alan Guttmacher Institute, the younger the teen mother is, the older her boyfriend tends to be. They warn that the typical scenario of a thirteen-year-old mother and twenty-five-year-old father "suggests, at the very least, very different levels of life experience and power, and brings into question issues of pressure and abuse."[13]

Some teens fall victim to sexual predators they meet online in Internet chat rooms.

Incest

Most young people count on being safe from sexual assault from their own family members. Tragically, that is not always the case. Young children may be victimized by family members who are pedophiles, people who are sexually attracted to children. Preteens and teenagers, most of whom are living at home as they go through puberty and physically mature, are also vulnerable to sexual abuse by family members. Experts estimate that one in every ten to twenty families may be involved in some form of incest, sexual contact between family members (for example, sibling/ sibling, father/daughter, or uncle/niece). About half of reported incest cases involve sexual intercourse.

Jeff was eleven the first time his older brother raped him. The abuse continued for three years. Jeff recalls: "Not only did he have intercourse with me, but he also made me perform oral sex on him. I tried several times to resist him but he was stronger than me. I cried every time he raped me, but he would never stop until he finished. I wanted to tell my mother but I didn't want to hurt her."[14]

No one knows for sure how many young people experience incest. Ashamed, humiliated, and fearful of the impact on their families, many victims do not tell anyone what is happening to them. As one twelve-year-old, who had been repeatedly raped by her father, explained: "My father told me that if I told my mother, they'd have to get a divorce and it would be my fault. He said my mother would blame me."[15]

Stranger rape

Stranger rape, in which the victim does not know his or her assailant, occurs in only a minority of cases. According to the National Council on Crime and Delinquency's study, *Our Vulnerable Teenagers: Their Victimization, Its Consequences, and Directions for Prevention and Intervention,* stranger rapes comprise an estimated 14 percent of attacks on female child and adolescent victims, with the percentage rising to nearly 20 percent for male victims. Young people who hitchhike or go out alone to secluded or sparsely populated places, particularly late at night, are at special risk for stranger rape.

For example, when seventeen-year-old Loren was in the Bahamas with a group of students from her high school, she decided to walk back to her hotel by herself after visiting a club one night. A local man grabbed her from behind, put a knife to the back of her neck, pushed her into the woods, and raped her. Afterward, he told her: "If you move or scream, I'm going to come back and slice you."[16] He then left and returned to check on her four or five times. Finally, he was gone. Loren waited several minutes, pulled on her shorts, and ran back to the hotel lobby where she collapsed.

When there is more than one attacker: gang rape

Gang rapes are sexual assaults perpetrated by multiple assailants. The U.S. Department of Justice estimates that one out of ten rapes involves more than one attacker. Most gang rapes are instigated by a teenage or young-adult male who is intent upon demonstrating his power and virility to his peers. Peers may participate because they fear the social stigma of refusing to join in. According to Chris O'Sullivan, a social psychologist who studied thirty-two campus gang rapes: "A lot of boys can't resist the peer pressure once they're in that group situation. If they won't participate in the sexual assault, they're called 'homos.' Their sexuality is ridiculed; that's very threatening."[17]

The instigator of a gang rape often targets an inexperienced, naïve, or intoxicated teenage victim. For example, Sara was just thirteen when she attended a graduation party in her small Texas town. After having several drinks, she agreed to take a ride with four older boys. "I asked them where we were going," Sara says, "and they told me just lay back and don't worry. I remember them laughing."[18] It turned out that where they were headed was a deserted country club golf course, where the boys took turns raping her.

Male teens are at the greatest risk for being victims of gang rape. Gang rape can leave lasting emotional and physical scars.

Male teens are at even greater risk for being victims of gang rapes and sustaining serious injuries. According to male-rape expert Cindy Struckman-Johnson, contrary to popular stereotypes, neither victims nor perpetrators of male rape are exclusively homosexual. In fact, close to two-thirds of victims and half of perpetrators of male rape are heterosexual.

Rape is a violent crime aimed at exerting power and control

Whether rape is perpetrated by a gang, a single dating partner, a casual acquaintance, a relative, or a stranger, it is a violent crime. The prevailing view among experts is that rape is motivated by the desire to overpower, control, and humiliate victims. Since teens, especially teenage girls, are at special risk, it is imperative to look at the underlying causes of rape.

2

The Causes of Rape

TEEN RAPES DO not occur in a social or cultural vacuum. The prevailing view among social scientists is that the root causes lie in the wider culture that condones or tolerates sexual aggression, particularly against women. Contributing factors include: the continued imbalance in power between men and women in society; a climate of disrespect toward women; the widespread portrayal of girls and women in the media as sex objects; the glorification of violence and the linking of sex and violence; widespread myths about rape; and gender-role socialization.

Moreover, research indicates that rape-supportive attitudes are notably prevalent in adolescent subculture. As they develop their own sexual identities, teenagers often feel anxious about their attractiveness and acceptability to peers. In response to their feelings of insecurity and uncertainty, some teens embrace rigid sex-role stereotypes that are associated with condoning or excusing rape.

Inequality and a climate of disrespect

Since the modern women's movement of the 1960s, there has been a significant increase in opportunities and roles for women in education and in the workplace. Men, however, continue to predominate in the upper levels of political and economic leadership, and women are still paid less than men for doing similar work.

Like other members of less-powerful groups in society, women are the frequent butt of put-downs, jokes, and other forms of disrespect. In general, a climate of disrespect toward

Female pop stars like Britney Spears are often marketed on the basis of their sexual attractiveness. Many social scientists believe that media portrayals of women as sex objects contribute to a climate of disrespect toward women.

women and their relative lack of power in society contribute to the tolerance of rape.

Nowhere is disrespect toward women more apparent than in the media, where females are frequently portrayed as sex objects. Young people who watch television and read magazines are exposed to thousands of advertisements that feature seductively dressed women selling alcohol, automobiles, and a host of other products. When teenagers shop at grocery or drug stores, they encounter prominent magazine-rack displays of soft-core pornography magazines such as *Playboy, Penthouse,* and *Hustler.* Moreover, as Martin D. Schwartz and Walter S. DeKeseredy point out in *Sexual Assault on the College Campus,* young people who watch movies and videos are regularly exposed to "the notion that women are meant to be semi-undressed sex objects, generally treated as inferior to men."[19]

Media glorification of violence and the linking of sex and violence

Research indicates that the more violent imagery a youth is exposed to, the more violence prone he or she is likely to become. For example, in a seventeen-year study led by Columbia University researcher Jeffrey Johnson, there was a fourfold increase in violence among teenagers who watched more than an hour of television a day compared to teens who watched less. Johnson concluded that imitation was a major factor: "We are social beings and we tend to want to try out things that we see other people doing, especially if we see the person rewarded for what they did or portrayed as a hero for it."[20] In addition, consistent with previous studies, Johnson's research indicated that young people who watch a lot of violence become used to it. "It has been shown that viewing media violence leads to a desensitization effect. The more violence that they see, the less negative, the more normal, it seems to them,"[21] says Johnson.

These findings are particularly significant because compared to previous generations, contemporary teenagers have been exposed to significantly more simulated violence and glorification of violence. Researchers estimate that by the age of eighteen, the average U.S. adolescent has witnessed approximately twenty-six thousand murders on television alone. Violent video games and action and horror films enjoy widespread popularity among young people.

According to sociologist Gail Dines-Levy of Boston's Wheelock College, "Sex and violence have become inextricably confused in the minds of young people."[22] Like many social scientists, she attributes much of the confusion to the negative impact of pop culture aimed at teen audiences, in which sex is repeatedly linked with violence. For example, music videos, lyrics, and album covers romanticize bondage and sexual assaults. Slasher films, widely available on cable TV and in video rental stores, feature graphic scenes of female mutilation, rape, and murder, and are staples of "gross-out" parties attended by eleven- to fifteen-year-olds.

The influence of rape myths

Rape myths are false beliefs about rape, rapists, and/or victims that are widely held and serve to deny or justify sexual aggression. As noted, a common myth is that a rapist is a deranged-looking stranger who attacks an unsuspecting victim. In fact, most rapists appear to be normal, rather ordinary individuals, and the vast majority of teen rape victims are raped by someone they know.

To the extent that teens buy into the myth that acquaintance rape does not constitute "real rape," they are less likely to be aware of the dangers of being victimized by an acquaintance, or the criminal liability involved in victimizing a peer. While media coverage of the growing body of research about rape in the past three decades has heightened awareness of acquaintance rape, researchers have uncovered considerable evidence that young people continue to resist defining their own experiences as rape. For example, in her research on acquaintance rape, Mary Koss found that only 27 percent of the young women whose sexual assault met the legal definition of rape thought of themselves as rape victims.

Although rapists are fully responsible for their criminal actions, a number of rape myths involve excusing the behav-

ior of rapists and blaming the victims instead. In fact, experts often point out that rape is the only crime in which the victim is routinely blamed. The person whose flashy sports car is stolen off the street while he is attending a raucous party is not apt to be blamed for its theft. A rape victim, however, is often accused of having "asked for it" by wearing provocative clothing, attending a party where alcohol and drugs are present, or placing herself in some other vulnerable situation. Sexually experienced (or rumored-to-be-experienced) girls, sexual "teases" (girls who agree to make out and then say "no" to sexual intercourse), girls who allow dates to spend a lot of money on them, or "uppity" girls who "need to be taught a lesson" may all be considered fair game.

Male attackers are considered less blameworthy. Beset with strong, overpowering sexual urges, sexually aggressive males who force sex are thought to have "gotten carried away and been unable to stop." In reality, males are perfectly capable of stopping when they are sexually excited, and research indicates that in most cases, the plan to rape or engage in sex (forced if necessary) is made ahead of time.

Many experts contend that the simulated violence in video games and movies has inured teens to actual violence.

Alcohol plays a large part in many rapes. Male rapists often justify their actions with the claim that alcohol impaired their better judgment.

Another related rape myth concerns drinking and involves a clear double standard for rapists and victims. Whereas drinking makes rape victims more culpable ("She brought it on herself by getting drunk"), it provides a ready-made excuse for rapists ("I was drunk, I didn't know what I was doing").

Minimizing the seriousness of rape

Minimizing the seriousness of sexual assault can lead teens to believe that forcing sex is not a violent crime. Instead, it is viewed as something young men sometimes do, a part of the journey to manhood in which "boys will be boys, sowing their wild oats." In a case that received extensive media coverage in 1993, a group of Lakewood, California, teenage boys who called themselves the Spur Posse were arrested for allegedly raping several girls as part of a sexual competition.

Donald Belman, one of the member's fathers, insisted it was all innocent fun: "Nothing my boy did was anything that any red-blooded American boy wouldn't do at his age."[23]

Rape is also discounted by claims that girls falsely "cry rape" to cover up their own promiscuous behavior or for revenge on former boyfriends or dates. Research indicates, however, that accusations of rape are rarely fabricated. Only 4 to 6 percent of sexual-assault cases stem from false accusations.

Rape is romanticized

Rape myths also romanticize rape as something women want and ultimately enjoy, even though they may have initially said "no" to avoid being perceived as too "loose." Statements such as "Some girls like it rough" and "Girls do not really mean it when they say 'no'" reflect the twin myths that rape is a romantic gesture and that girls really mean "yes" when they say "no." A number of researchers have pointed to the media as being partially responsible for popularizing these myths. In the classic film *Gone with the Wind,* Scarlett O'Hara happily hums and smiles the morning after being forcibly carried up the stairs and presumably raped by Rhett Butler. Since its 1939 release, thousands of film and television scripts, not to mention "bodice ripper" novels, have reiterated the message that rape is romantic and that women enjoy being raped.

Many teens do not subscribe to these myths about rape, yet several research studies indicate that a disturbing number, particularly teenage boys, believe them. For example, when Dr. Jacqueline Goodchilds and colleagues from the University of California published their landmark study of more than four hundred teens in 1988, they reported that only 20 percent of teens felt that forced sex was never acceptable. More than half of the boys and a quarter of the girls thought it was "okay" for a guy to force a girl who has led him on to have sex with him. Fifty-one percent of the boys and 42 percent of the girls thought it was okay if the girl had gotten him sexually excited, while 43 percent of the boys and 32 percent of the girls thought it was okay if the couple had dated for a long time.

Blaming the victim

Research also indicates that many teens partially or fully blame rape victims if they have been dressed provocatively. In Ruth Kershner's study of high school students, 46 percent of respondents believed that some girls encourage rape by the way they dress, and 53 percent agreed that "some women provoke men into raping them."[24] When Susan K. Telljohann studied high school students' perceptions of nonconsensual sexual activity, only one in three students thought that a girl who dressed sexy and got raped was not partially responsible for the incident. Sixty percent of the eighth graders in another study agreed with the statement, "When women go around braless or wearing short skirts and tight tops, they are just asking for trouble."[25]

Rape victims who were wearing provocative clothing at the time of the incident often find themselves being blamed for the crime.

As one teenage girl described, the tendency to blame the victim of sexual assault is commonplace: "They always blame the girl, like what she was wearing, or she's sexually active, so she must be a whore, or she's making it up just to get a guy in trouble." [26]

Gender-role socialization in a male-dominated society

Dramatic differences in how boys and girls are traditionally raised have been cited as a factor contributing to rape. Girls are socialized to be friendly, put the feelings and needs of others first, and avoid offending anyone by asserting themselves. As a result, many girls find it more difficult to assertively resist sexual assaults. As one teenage rape victim explained: "I never considered punching him or doing something really drastic. I guess I was a 'nice girl' and you didn't do that, even if somebody was un-nice to you." [27]

In contrast, boys are steered onto what researchers Robin Warshaw and Andrea Parrot call an "aggression track" [28] in which they learn to disregard the needs and feelings of others, use force to beat an opponent in a conflict, and equate showing empathy with being weak and "girlish." In a society in which women are routinely viewed as sex objects, this type of training contributes to the belief that sexual assault is an acceptable behavior. In discussing acquaintance rape, Schwartz and DeKeseredy summarize this point of view: "Only a male-dominated society that trains men to use women as objects, and that legitimizes violence as a tool to achieve personal goals with a callous indifference to the feelings of victimized others, could breed a large number of men who openly assault women they know, and, in fact, may even like." [29]

The exaggeration of gender-role stereotypes in adolescent subculture

As adolescents differentiate from parents and forge an independent identity and direction in life, relationships with friends assume increasing importance. The longing for peer acceptance is nearly universal and contributes to teens' willingness to conform to stereotypes and keep silent about the issue of rape.

In combination with the ceaseless exposure to gender stereotypical models in the media, the insecurity of adolescence results in peer pressure among many teens to behave in exaggeratedly stereotypical ways. Boys are "supposed to be" aggressive and macho, while girls are supposed to be compliant, passive, and above all "nice." As Robin Warshaw notes, a visitor to any junior high or high school is likely to meet a lot of young people who "show rigid adherence to the doctrines of hypermasculinity and female sexual socialization."[30]

The pressure to "score" for boys

A major aspect of the macho expectations for boys involves being sexually aggressive and successfully "scoring" (engaging in sexual intercourse). As Mike Weber, a member of the Spur Posse group in Lakewood, California, explained about their sexual competition: "If you had sex, you got a point. It was like bragging rights for the person who thought he was the biggest stud."[31]

Numerous researchers and observers have noted that this is an aspect of adolescent subculture that has remained remarkably unchanged. Like their fathers, many young men report that they feel pressure (especially from their male friends) to see "how far" they can go. Making a sexual conquest is widely perceived as a way of affirming masculinity.

For insecure adolescents, the pressure to demonstrate masculinity through sexually aggressive behavior may have much to do with the dynamics of gang rape as well. According to Michael Kimmel, a sociologist at the State University of New York at Stony Brook, a lot of adolescent gang rape "takes place when there's one guy who wants to prove he's a man and five guys who are terrified of being thought of as less than one."[32]

Conflicting sexuality messages and pressures for teenage girls

Teenage girls, meanwhile, are subjected to conflicting messages and pressures about sexual activity. On the one

hand, many girls are raised to be the "gatekeepers" of sexual activity. For moral reasons, as well as to avoid premature pregnancy and sexually transmitted diseases, they are admonished to resist going "too far" with boys. Moreover, girls quickly become aware of the risk of damaging their reputation by becoming sexually active. Unlike males, who enjoy increased social status by virtue of sexual activity, sexually active girls are in danger of being labeled "sluts."

Adolescent girls are also, however, bombarded with media images of sex as hip and fashionable and are often the subject of peer pressure to become sexually active. As therapist Mary Pipher observes in *Reviving Ophelia*:

> In the halls of junior highs, girls are pressured to be sexual
> regardless of the quality of relationships. Losing virginity is

Peer pressure and insecurity play major roles in teen rape. Boys often feel pressured to act sexually aggressive, while insecure girls sometimes feel compelled to accept sexual advances.

considered a rite of passage into maturity. Girls may be encouraged to have sex with boys they hardly know. Many girls desperate for approval succumb to this pressure. But unfortunately the double standard still exists. The same girls who are pressured to have sex on Saturday night are called sluts on Monday morning. The boys who coaxed them into sex at the parties avoid them in the halls at school. [33]

Secondary school hallways are also places where sexual harassment is flourishing. In a study of eighth- through eleventh-grade students sponsored by the American Association of University Women Educational Foundation, 80 percent of students reported experiencing harassment at school, ranging from being touched or grabbed in a sexual way, to being taunted, to having others spread sexual rumors about them. When Dr. Jill Murray visited local high schools to talk about abusive dating relationships, she discovered that "boys didn't think that pushing a girl against a wall or grabbing her face or breasts was abusive—it was merely an attention-getting device." [34]

This kind of rampant sexual aggressiveness and harassment can all too easily escalate into rape. Moreover, many teachers and school officials implicitly condone sexually aggressive behavior by dismissing it as adolescent pranks or awkward attempts at sexual teasing. As one young woman who was raped by her boyfriend at fifteen recalls: "Teachers saw him shoving me and yanking me around and verbally putting me down. They just accepted it as puppy love and did nothing to stop it." [35]

Abuse in dating relationships

Many girls feel enormous pressure to acquire boyfriends and hold on to them as a way of ensuring or advancing their social status. This can leave them vulnerable to being coerced into having unwanted sex. In her research, Susan K. Telljohann and her colleagues found evidence that teenage girls believed that if they engaged in sexual intercourse, they could keep their boyfriends interested in them.

Inexperienced at dating, some teens mistakenly interpret extreme jealousy, possessiveness, and a dating partner's attempts to control and dominate them as signs of love and commitment, instead of abuse. Tragically, they may even encounter pressure from peers to stay in these relationships. Nancy Worcester reports: "Many young women have said that even when they told friends they were being hurt by their boyfriends, the response was that they were lucky to have boyfriends. There is enormous peer pressure not to break up."[36]

Less parental supervision and guidance

With the increase in single-parent and two-career families, many adolescents also receive less parental supervision and guidance about how to treat other people and what constitutes healthy, respectful behavior in dating relationships. Moreover, in a rapidly changing, diverse, highly sexualized society complicated by conflicting norms about sexuality, there is less consensus than in previous generations about what sexual behavioral guidelines to impart to young people. It is interesting that Eric Richardson, a member of the Spur Posse group, told a reporter: "They pass out condoms, teach sex education and pregnancy this and pregnancy that. But they don't teach us any rules."[37]

While aspects of the wider culture and adolescent subculture, and the decreased presence of adult supervision and guidance in teenagers' lives, create a climate conducive to rape, the majority of teenagers do not rape or get raped. To better understand the dynamics of teen rape, it is important to examine what factors make some teens more vulnerable than others.

3

Risk Factors for Rape

TEEN RAPE CUTS across class, racial, ethnic, gender, sexual orientation, religious, and geographic boundaries. No one is immune from the risk of rape. Some teens, however, are at greater risk than others. Researchers have identified several interrelated factors that increase vulnerability both to the risk of raping and being raped. Of these factors, family dynamics play a pivotal role.

The impact of childhood abuse

One of the most striking findings in the research literature is the link between childhood sexual abuse and the risk of continued and repeated sexual victimization as an adolescent and adult. Why is this so? Experiencing sexual abuse is devastating to a child's developing sense of self and sexual esteem and often leads to depression and to a host of self-destructive behaviors, including substance abuse and premature sexual experimentation and promiscuity. Drug and alcohol use and promiscuity, in turn, have been linked to greater risk of later sexual victimization.

Childhood sexual abuse may also leave teens without the skills to say "no" and increase the chances of being sexually passive partners. Offering no resistance may have helped victims survive childhood abuse with a minimum of violence but may leave them vulnerable to repeated victimization as teens and adults. According to psychologist Judith S. Musick, "An abusive childhood experience affects the capacity to make responsible choices, including whether to have sex, and whether to have protected sex."[38] In fact, there is a significant link between sexual abuse, rape, and teen pregnancy. In a study in Illinois, more than 60 percent of the teenage mothers surveyed admitted to being sexually abused as a child or being forced to have sex as a teen.

As noted, teen rape often takes place in the context of an ongoing abusive dating relationship, and the evidence is that teens who have been sexually abused as children are particularly vulnerable to becoming involved with abusive partners. In *Reviving Ophelia,* Mary Pipher talks about one of her clients, fifteen-year-old Terra, who had been sexually abused by her stepgrandfather as a child and was now

Females raped or sexually abused in their childhood have a heightened risk of becoming teenage mothers.

involved with a boyfriend who regularly tied her up and forced her to have sex with him:

> Terra reminded me of many young women who were abused as children. Often they must rework the abuse when they are teenagers. They're all mixed up about love, sex, punishment and affection. They need to erase memories of bad relationships and build ideas about good ones. Otherwise they are at risk of finding boyfriends like the person who abused them. [39]

Adolescents with an abusive home life are also more likely to become runaways, which dramatically increases their vulnerability to becoming victims of both sexual and physical violence. According to the National Council on Crime and Delinquency's report, *Our Vulnerable Teenagers,* adolescents who are sexually and/or physically abused in the home are much more likely to run away, become homeless, and turn to deviant survival activities such as prostitution or selling drugs. These activities, in turn, increase their risk of revictimization.

Experiencing abuse at home also increases vulnerability to becoming a rapist. According to Susan Xenarios, director of St. Luke's–Roosevelt Hospital Rape Intervention Project in New York City: "Many juvenile offenders probably witnessed or were victims of some sort of sexual abuse and are acting out their anger. If the child's father is violent, the son will often mirror his behavior." [40]

Even when teens themselves were not abused as children, witnessing abuse can leave them vulnerable to the assumption that violence, including sexual violence, is expected in intimate relationships. When teenagers observe male partners abusing their mothers, they are much more likely to perceive that this kind of male/female relationship is normal.

Traditional roles and attitudes within the family

Parents who adhere to traditional roles in their intimate relationships may inadvertently increase their offspring's vulnerability to rape. If teen girls, for example, are brought up to believe that males are in charge and it is a woman's obligation to sexually satisfy her partner and uncomplain-

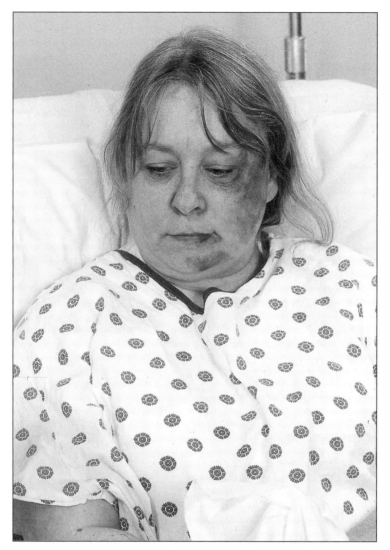

Males who grow up with abused mothers like this woman are at increased risk of becoming abusers themselves.

ingly make herself available to his desires, they can be at much greater risk for rape and other abuse within their dating relationships.

Despite being raised in a middle-class home, Debbie Mattson talks about the cost of growing up in a household where women were not considered equal to men:

> I do believe . . . the reason I stayed in an abusive relationship as a young teenager is that I was taught that girls were inferior to boys. I certainly felt that opportunities were much more limited for girls in comparison to those for boys. And I did feel

at a loss about where I belonged because my "tomboy" behavior was constantly being disapproved of by peers, teachers, parents and other adults. [41]

To the extent that girls have internalized the message that they should defer to men, avoid making scenes, or fail to stand up for themselves even in dangerous situations, they are at greater risk for rape. In research comparing successful and unsuccessful resisters of rape, successful resisters were more confident, assertive, and clearer in their communications.

Traditional attitudes and roles within the family can also increase the likelihood of becoming a rapist. Investigative journalist Michelle Stacey notes that numerous psychologists believe that how a young man is raised has a great deal to do with how prone to rape he will become. "For instance," says Stacey, "a father who suggests to his son that women are adversaries and sexual objects, that his role is to trick or pressure girls into having sex—or even a father who demonstrates by belittling his wife that he has little respect for women—may help set the stage for later sexual assaults." [42]

Attitudes of rapists

In fact, research on young rapists indicates that what sets them apart from nonassaultive males is their more wholehearted embrace of macho attitudes and beliefs. They are significantly more likely to hold callous attitudes toward girls and accept rape-supportive beliefs. They also tend to hold more rigid and stereotyped ideas of male and female roles. Many sexually and physically abusive boyfriends, says Dr. Jill Murray, reveal their beliefs in male superiority "by making demeaning comments about women in general, or speaking of women as chicks, babes, or broads." [43]

Studies also reveal that sexually aggressive males are less empathetic toward the needs and feelings of others and tend to behave immaturely, irresponsibly, and, at times, aggressively. In describing her abusive high school boyfriend, Jan K. Jenson recalls: "He frequently got into fights with the other guys, sometimes physical fights. I remember seeing him shove people out of his way and up against the lockers as he walked down the hallways at school."[44]

It is important to note, however, that rapists can also be very charming and likable. Many excel in school, are good-looking, and are well liked, even admired, by their peers. Murray says that abusive boyfriends often have a dual personality, and that many use their charisma "as a ploy to enter a girl's life and keep her parents from being suspicious of him."[45]

The impact of paternal absence or neglect

Teen girls whose fathers are not actively involved in their lives often hunger for male attention and are at risk for premature sexual experimentation, promiscuity, and sexual victimization. LeVonda, whose father was in prison for sexually molesting her older sisters, spoke of her search for male affection: "I guess since I've never had a male role model, I kept looking to guys for comfort. My sophomore year, I had sex with about ten guys. Then I started dating Tyler, who raped me repeatedly and beat me. Afterward, he'd apologize and be real nice, and I'd want to believe he would change, and it would be different next time. But it never was."[46]

The search for a substitute father figure may also contribute to vulnerability to sexually predatory older boyfriends. In a study on teen pregnancy, Child Trends, a Washington, D.C.–based research organization, concluded that preteen and early-teen girls were at greatest risk for sexual abuse and rape by older boyfriends. Nearly 40 percent of thirteen- and fourteen-year-old girls reported their first sexual experience was unwanted. For those who had sex younger than thirteen, the figure rose to more than 70 percent.

Father absence or neglect is also a significant risk factor for male victims of rape. Adult offenders typically get close to boys starved for male attention with disarming gestures of praise, attention, and interest. Often, these older men are in positions of trust and authority. They may, for example, be teachers, coaches, family friends, clergy, or relatives.

The relationship between fathers and children is crucial with regard to rape prevention. Children who lack male role models often become victims or perpetrators of violence.

In addition, father absence or neglect may increase the likelihood of engaging in sexual assault and other deviant behavior. Numerous researchers have found that young boys who grow up with absent or uninvolved fathers often fail to develop a healthy sense of masculinity and may look to their neighborhood street gang for companionship, acceptance, and a sense of masculine identity.

The power of peers

If the neighborhood street gang or peer group endorses violence against women as a way of demonstrating masculinity and bonding as males, the likelihood that their members will commit rape increases. The support of peers, particularly for teenagers, can be a significant factor. Schwartz and DeKeseredy review a number of research studies that provide evidence of the impact of peers. In one study, for example, more than 40 percent of adolescent perpetrators of sexual assault reported that their friends knew about their behavior and that virtually all approved of it, or at least expressed indifference.

Research also indicates that the peers of rapists are more apt to be sexually abusive themselves. Sexual abusers are significantly more likely to have friends who had forced young women (or tried to force them) to have sex with them after the women refused. They also reported having more friends who had gotten women high on drugs or drunk in order to have sex with them. Not surprisingly, these sexually abusive males were also significantly more prone to heavy alcohol use.

Evidence indicates that on college campuses, fraternities and athletic teams are among the most common settings in which sexually abusive peer groups flourish. For example, in one study, although only 25 percent of the male students on campus were fraternity members, they accounted for 63 percent of the sexual assaults. In another study at a large midwestern university, although male athletes made up less than 2 percent of the male population on campus, they represented 23 percent of the men accused of sexual assault.

Peer relationships are especially important to teenagers. The peers of a rapist are apt to be sexually abusive themselves.

Why should this be the case? Athletes, whose exploits on and off the playing field are celebrated by the media and whose criminal behavior is the subject of an entire website called the Sports Hall of Shame, may perceive that society's rules do not fully apply to them. As sociologist John Murphy points out, athletes in our sports-obsessed society receive special privileges and protection: "High school and college athletes aren't held responsible for their grades, their actions. Someone's always taking care of them."[47] Not having been held accountable for their actions, athletes may believe that they can get away with sexual assault. There may also be some spillover effect on off-court behavior from being involved in a physically aggressive competitive sport where there is a heavy emphasis on winning, scoring, and often, humiliating and crushing opponents.

Even more significant, however, say Schwartz and De-Keseredy, is that when males band together strongly in groups that exclude women, they are more likely to see women as what they call "Other."[48] Discussions about girls in these male-only groups tend to center upon stories of sexual exploits, how to "get" sex from women, and how to control or dominate women. In addition to providing support for the idea that "real men have sex on demand," there is an emphasis in these groups on secrecy and loyalty, which keeps males from revealing the sexually violent behavior of their fellow members to outsiders. Since no one will tell, there are often no consequences and, thus, an absence of deterrence.

Similar dynamics may operate in gang rapes perpetrated by street gangs and other tightly bonded male groups. According to psychologist Bernice Sandler, young males who engage in gang rape "are raping for each other. The woman is incidental."[49]

Peers are also a significant factor affecting the risk of becoming a victim of rape. Teenage girls whose friends are in abusive relationships are more likely to get into and remain in dangerous relationships themselves.

Low self-esteem

Concerns about peer acceptance may also play a role in increasing teenage girls' vulnerability to sexual assault and exploitation. In discussing the victims of the Spur Posse gang, Robert C. Ripley, commander of the Los Angeles County Sheriff's Department, sadly reported: "These were 14- and 15-year-old girls who were unsure of themselves and wanted to be liked."[50]

Young women with low self-esteem are particularly vulnerable to peer pressure. LeVonda recalls that the beginning of her sexual torments occurred during the summer she turned twelve: "I started hanging out with these three girls. Everyday, they tormented me for being a virgin. After a while, everyone in the neighborhood knew, and I was constantly harassed by all of my peers. I got sick and tired of being made fun of, and I finally did it with this 16-year-old guy. I hated every minute of it."[51]

Adolescents with disabilities are at risk

Adolescents with developmental disabilities, especially those in the mildly retarded range, are at special risk for rape and other forms of abuse. An estimated 50 to 80 percent of people with developmental disabilities have been sexually or physically abused and are vulnerable both to date rape and abuse by caregivers and others in authority.

Often, disabled teens have been taught to be acquiescent and may have difficulty differentiating between appropriate and inappropriate touch, leading, in some cases, to victimization as extreme as rape. In 2000, for example, eighteen men allegedly gang-raped a mentally disabled thirteen-year-old girl in Marietta, Georgia.

Rapists may target teens with disabilities because they believe their chances of getting away with rape are better with disabled victims. Not only are rapists apt to assume that disabled teens would offer less resistance, but they may believe that disabled victims' recollections and testimony about an attack would be unreliable.

Situational risk factors

While a troubled background, low self-esteem, or a disability can increase a teen's vulnerability to rape, many teen rape victims do not suffer from any of these problems. They are assertive, come from loving homes, and feel good about themselves prior to their being assaulted. In fact, some experts think it is much more useful to look at the characteristics of situations that predict sexual aggression, rather than the personalities and backgrounds of victims.

What are key situational risk factors? Certainly, drinking and taking drugs significantly increase vulnerability to rape. Alcohol and drugs loosen inhibitions, dull common sense, and make it harder to use good judgment. According to the American Academy of Pediatrics, more than 40 percent of adolescent rape victims and rapists report that they were drinking or using drugs immediately before a sexual assault.

In some cases, a rape victim is drugged by his or her assailant. For example, here is the story of what happened to eighteen-year-old Jenny when she went to Florida on spring break with a girlfriend. On the first day of vacation, Jenny and her friend met two guys on the beach. "We played volleyball with them, and they seemed really nice,"[52] recalls Jenny. When the boys invited the girls to come to their hotel that night for a party, they eagerly accepted.

At the party, Jenny felt a little uncomfortable. Her friend left with a guy she met, and everyone was drinking beer. Jenny hated beer, so she asked for a Coke. One of the boys went to the kitchen to pour her drink and then brought it out to her. Jenny took a few sips and within minutes, felt dizzy and weak. She vaguely remembers that the boy who had brought her the Coke guided her into one of the back bedrooms to lie down. Then she passed out. When she woke up several hours later, her pants were pulled down around her ankles, and she was sore and bleeding in her vaginal area. Horrified, Jenny realized that she had been raped. But she felt so groggy and confused, she could not remember what had happened.

The boy who had fixed Jenny a Coke had slipped a date-rape drug called Rohypnol, also known as roofies, into her drink. Rohypnol is a tasteless, odorless, and colorless sedative that has devastating effects. It can blur victims' vision and make them feel paralyzed. Some people black out and cannot remember anything that happened to them while under the drug's influence.

Drinking alcohol or taking drugs increases a teen's risk of becoming a victim of rape or a perpetrator of the crime.

Rohypnol, along with two other date-rape drugs, GHB and Ketamine, make rape much easier to accomplish. The victim is not only temporarily incapacitated but cannot clearly recall the attack. Moreover, these drugs move quickly through the body and often cannot be detected in blood or urine tests by the time a victim gets to the hospital.

Date-rape drugs first became available in the early 1990s and have been especially popular on high school and college campuses, predominantly in Florida, California, and Texas, where they enter the country via Mexico or Colombia. Despite their illegality, they are widely available and pose a special risk to unsuspecting teens and adults.

Lack of control of circumstances

Research indicates that teen girls are also at greater risk for date rape when they go out on dates initiated and paid for by males and on outings for which their dates do the driving. Sexually aggressive males may feel entitled to sex in exchange for the effort and money they have expended. In addition, by doing the driving, they have control over the activity and location and may choose an isolated location, such as the beach or a deserted road.

In general, agreeing to accompany someone to an area where no one else will be around, such as an unoccupied home, empty dorm room, or secluded spot, places a teen at greater risk for sexual assault. Opening the door to a stranger, walking alone at night, hitchhiking, and agreeing to ride in cars with strangers all increase vulnerability to stranger rape.

If a teen feels uncomfortable, rape victims and counselors strongly advise leaving a situation immediately. Often, they say, an attack can successfully be avoided by paying attention to gut instincts. Ann, for example, became uncomfortable when she arrived at her friend Dave's house to help him make invitations for a party. There were no lights on in the house, and Dave greeted her wearing only tight gray sweatpants and no shirt: "This little voice inside my head was telling me: Something's wrong with this picture,"[53] Ann recalls. However, she kept telling herself that Dave and she were just friends, and dismissed her worries. She paid dearly for ignoring her gut feelings. Once she had entered Dave's house, he raped her.

Whatever the situation in which a rape takes place, rapists are likely to subscribe to the myths that rape is no big deal and that, anyway, girls enjoy being raped. Those who have experienced rape, or who have studied or worked with rape victims, however, paint a very different picture of the impact of rape.

4

The Impact of Rape

AT ANY AGE or stage in life, rape is a traumatic, degrading, and humiliating experience. It destroys a sense of personal safety and brings into question basic assumptions about oneself and the wider world. Many experts maintain that when rape happens to teenagers, the experience is especially devastating. This is because adolescents are in the process of formulating their basic belief systems, personal identities, and attitudes and feelings about authority figures, gender roles, and relationships.

Acquaintance rape, by far the most common type of teen rape, is especially traumatic. As rape researcher Barry Burkhart points out: "To be raped is to be exposed to the ultimate assault on one's dignity, value, and power of self-determination. To be raped by someone you trusted and often selected to date is to be betrayed, not just by the perpetrator, but by your own judgment." [54]

As noted, many teens subscribe to rape myths, in which acquaintance rape is not perceived as "real rape." Instead, assaults are minimized as incidents that apparently "got out of hand," and for which victims are largely to blame. Confused about whether what happened to them was actually rape, and concerned about the reactions of family and friends, teen rape victims are the least likely to seek help and the most likely to suffer in silence from acute feelings of self-blame, guilt, and shame. After Ann was raped by her friend Dave at his house, she recalls:

> I was in shock. I went home, went to my room and didn't talk to anyone. I felt as though if anyone had known what had just

happened, they would think that I'd led him on. I couldn't tell anyone what had happened. What would they think of me? I grew up in a really nice neighborhood, and Dave's family was so well-known. I thought if I talked about it, it would just bring shame to me and my family. I felt that *I* was the bad person, that somehow I had brought this on, that I had asked for it. [55]

Ashamed that they were unable to stave off an attack, and irrationally fearful that being raped may mean that they are homosexual, male victims are even less likely to tell anyone about their experience. Some experts estimate that whereas the figure for reporting rape is one in ten for female victims, it is closer to one in one hundred for male victims.

Secondary victimization

When teens do reveal that they have been raped, many family members and friends offer strong support and comfort. Unfortunately, others, influenced by widely held rape myths, may blame and doubt the victim. Their reactions may further hurt and traumatize a rape victim and amount to what experts call a secondary victimization. For example, sixteen-year-old Kristi, who was drugged and raped by a boy she met while vacationing in Florida, wept as she recalled her mother's reaction: "Well, what did you expect? How could you be so stupid as to agree to go to a party with someone you barely knew?" [56]

Sometimes friends, especially girlfriends, may deny the rape happened or blame the victim's behavior for having caused the rape ("This never would have happened if you had not been drinking, worn that outfit, gone to his house," etc.), as a way to preserve their own sense of safety. It is too frightening to think that rape could happen to them, so instead they distance themselves by telling themselves, "I would never do/say/wear that so I won't be raped."

Boyfriends may also have a tough time when their girlfriends are raped. Influenced by rape myths, they may feel angry, confused, and wonder whether their girlfriends were somehow at fault. They may also be struggling to handle

their girlfriends' extreme emotional distress and intense reactions after an assault.

Even when family and loved ones are making every effort to be supportive, they are traumatized as well. When Stephen Schmidt's sixteen-year-old daughter was raped walking home from her part-time job, he recalls being wracked by his sense of failure to protect her: "My own adult fatherly world seemed shattered, and I wondered if the center would hold. I was afraid, then angry, hate-filled and violent. I felt gratitude that she was alive. Mostly, I felt helpless." [57]

Not surprisingly, the distress of family and friends contributes to the distress of rape victims. As therapist Rebecca

Family members who blame or doubt a rape victim often inflict further trauma, a situation known as secondary victimization.

Campbell points out: "Rape survivors may be struggling not only with their own reactions to the assault, but also with how it is affecting those close to them."[58]

In some cases, relationships are destroyed. When the rapist is a friend or family member, loved ones caught in loyalty conflicts may side with the assailant and either refuse to believe the victim or blame the victim. For example, after thirteen-year-old Cherise pressed rape charges against her best friend's uncle, her best friend stopped speaking to her and was furious "for getting her uncle in trouble, even though she knew what he had done."[59]

In fact, it is common for the supporters of rapists to blame and harass victims, particularly if they report the rape and press charges. When thirteen-year-old Sara told authorities that she had been gang-raped by three senior boys, including a star quarterback and star baseball player, she was mercilessly attacked by the boys' supporters. Girls from the senior class filled her answering machine with obscene messages. Kids drove by her house and shouted obscenities. Others came at night and wrapped the place in toilet paper.

Likewise, when Lyndsey, a high school freshman, decided to press charges against two popular boys who had deliberately gotten her drunk and taken turns raping her, she endured intense harassment at school: "People started saying that I wanted it, or that since I went to the party and got drunk, it was my own fault. One girl beat me up and called me a slut; other kids wrote nasty things on my locker, including DP, for 'double penetration.' I still hear people whispering about 'what Lyndsey did' as I walk down the school hallways."[60]

While significant progress has been made in the legal system with regard to the treatment of rape victims and the prosecution of rapists, survivors who file charges can still expect to feel as though they themselves are on trial. Despite the proliferation of rape shield laws, designed to protect victims from having irrelevant details of their sexual history paraded before juries, the most common defense strategy in acquaintance rape cases remains attacking the character and credibility of the accuser. Investigative reporter Maria

Alvarez says that during the highly publicized rape trial of Alex, a former high school wrestler, his victim Adrienne endured insinuations in court that "as a large, athletic girl, she could have fought off the wrestling champ if she had really wanted to, implications that she was merely feeling 'Catholic guilt' about voluntarily sleeping with Alex, and accusations of having been drunk and high the night of the rape."[61]

When it is a case in which the verdict comes down to his word versus hers, the widespread prevalence of rape myths often results in juries siding with the accused rather than the victim. After spending hours testifying about the most intimate details of her rape by an abusive ex-boyfriend, only to have him found not guilty, Me Ra Koh says: "I had been told that going through the legal process would feel like being raped a second time, but actually it was worse."[62]

Rape trauma syndrome

Given the traumatic nature of rape and its aftermath, it is not surprising that an estimated 80 percent of adolescent rape victims suffer a reaction to rape that is called rape trauma syndrome or, more generally, posttraumatic stress disorder (PTSD). Initially, survivors are typically in a state of shock or disbelief. Some respond by being very expressive. They may cry, scream, swear, shout, or laugh nervously. Others appear numb and unusually calm and composed. Both reactions are normal.

Often, a victim wants to bathe or shower. Me Ra Koh recalls: "I was in shock. All I remember about those following hours is standing in the shower with all my clothes on, sobbing uncontrollably, desperately wanting the water to wash away the evening's events."[63]

Following the shock and disbelief, survivors typically experience a variety of emotions. Guilt and self-blame are apt to set in almost immediately. Victims may also feel angry, frightened, humiliated, ashamed, dirty, vengeful, and degraded. They may be jumpy and startle easily. Most have recurring nightmares and flashbacks about the attack and may have trouble sleeping, eating, and concentrating. Often, their schoolwork suffers. When Georgette, an eighteen-year-old college freshman, was raped by one of the resident assistants in her dormitory, she says:

> There's no way to describe what was going on inside me. I was losing control and I'd never been so terrified and helpless in my life. I felt as if my whole world had been kicked out from under me and I had been left to drift all alone in the darkness. I had horrible nightmares in which I relived the rape and others which were even worse. I was terrified of being with people and terrified of being alone. I couldn't concentrate on anything and began failing several classes.[64]

Teen rape survivors typically exhibit a variety of emotions, have nightmares and flashbacks, and experience trouble concentrating in school.

In the months that follow a rape, mood swings and irritability are common. Lyndsey says that ever since she was raped by two boys nine months ago, "I blow up at my brother and sister a lot, and I get sad for no reason."[65]

Sometimes a panic attack or a painful flashback is triggered by a scent, a sound, a touch, or a situation reminiscent of the rape. Vicki says that even two years after her rape at seventeen, "there are times when, if someone touches me or calls out my name in a certain way, I freak out. That will be with me always."[66]

Many victims become depressed, anxious, withdrawn, and feel worthless. According to the National Center for Injury Prevention and Control, compared to nonvictims, victims of date rape are eleven times more likely to be clinically depressed and six times more likely to experience social phobias. In their research on high school students, Christine Gidycz and Mary Koss found that nearly 50 percent of victims experienced suicidal thoughts, compared to only 7 percent of nonvictims. Almost 20 percent of adolescent rape victims who do not receive mental health counseling make actual suicide attempts.

Elizabeth, who was gang-raped at eighteen after having been molested between twelve and sixteen by a cousin, speaks to the intense pain and hopelessness that many victims experience: "Sometimes I feel like ending it all. . . . I have no more pride in who I am. Really, what am I? Did I 'ask for it'? Will life go on? Will I ever trust people? Will the pain ever go away?"[67]

The difficulty teen rape victims often have in trusting other people affects their social lives and emotional adjustment dramatically. Georgiana Bak, the mother of Adrienne, a teenage rape victim, said that the rape had changed her child from a "vivacious, outgoing girl into a withdrawn, scared, and emotionally devastated person."[68]

Avoidance

A common reaction of victims is to attempt to avoid situations even remotely reminiscent of the rape experience. They may change schools, friendship groups, and may withdraw

Many victims avoid emotional intimacy in the immediate aftermath of the crime, spending a lot of time alone.

altogether from social situations. After her rape, Adrienne avoided going on dates during high school. When she finally went to her senior prom, and her date tried to kiss her, she refused to see him again.

Many victims avoid intimacy and report long-term difficulties feeling comfortable in sexual relationships. Seven years after being raped on a date during her freshman year of college, Jacqueline says: "Before I wasn't tense about loving. I was more giving. Much more trusting. I don't know how to give anymore. I don't like sex. I don't like to be touched. I felt like I was a whore if I enjoyed sex."[69]

Denial

In their efforts to cope with the trauma of rape and protect their loved ones, many victims attempt to deny either that the rape happened or that it had a significant impact upon them. After thirteen-year-old Cherise was raped, for example, she recalls initially refusing counseling, and trying to be strong and brave to comfort her parents and "make them believe that nothing was wrong with me."[70]

Male victims, for whom the stigmatization and humiliation associated with rape may be even greater, often cope by denying the reality of the experience. According to researchers Cheryl Black and Richard DeBlassie, adult male mental health clients are particularly likely to repress and deny childhood and adolescent rape and sexual abuse.

Self-destructive behaviors

One of the most tragic repercussions of rape is that victims' anger and distress are often turned inward and result in self-destructive, risky behaviors. In addition to significantly greater vulnerability to depression and suicide, rape victims are at much greater risk for smoking, developing eating disorders, and cutting and injuring themselves. According

Angry and distressed, some rape victims engage in self-destructive behaviors such as smoking.

to the National Center for Injury Prevention and Control, they are also two and a half times more likely to abuse drugs and alcohol than nonvictims. The prevailing view among experts is that many of these behaviors stem from attempts to self-medicate and cope with emotional pain.

Cherise, for example, blamed herself for being raped. Convinced that she was somehow a bad person, she began cutting herself about a month after the attack: "I just wanted to change the way I was hurting. By making myself hurt physically, I could make myself feel better emotionally."[71] When cutting was not enough to relieve her pain, she began running away from home, hanging out with drug-using friends, and experimenting with drugs. At the age of fifteen, she dropped out of high school.

Victims are also at significantly greater risk for sexual promiscuity. Lisa, who was raped at thirteen by her best friend's cousin at a party, says: "After the rape, my life was devastated. I was so hurt and ashamed about what happened . . . I started getting really rebellious and hanging out with the wrong sort of kids. I started acting loose. I felt so cheap and dirty, as if I didn't deserve anything better for myself."[72]

Long-term effects

Even after several years, survivors are more likely to suffer from major depression, substance abuse, PTSD, a lack of interest in sex, and physical complaints such as headaches and stomach pains. Moreover, the risk of revictimization is significant. Research indicates that women who were raped before age sixteen are three and a half times more likely to become victims of domestic violence and almost three times as likely to be raped as adults.

Despite the devastating impact of rape, however, many teen victims do recover, gaining or regaining a strong sense of self-confidence and the ability to maintain healthy, positive relationships. The recovery process first depends on facing the experience.

5

Recovering from Rape

MANY TEEN RAPE victims initially assume that they will be able to get over the trauma by themselves. They do not even want to think or talk about the assault. Their reaction to the painful experience is to forget the rape and, it is hoped, put it behind them.

Unfortunately, not talking to anyone about a traumatic experience makes recovery much more difficult. Thirteen-year-old Lisa says that she did not begin to feel better until she began sharing what had happened to her with other people: "I urge any girl who is raped to talk about it with people—preferably an adult—you trust. Get out that awful secret. Because if you don't, it will only fester inside of you and cause you more and more pain."[73]

Immediate responses

Getting attention, care, and support right away helps the healing process begin and maximizes the chances of making a successful recovery. Many teen victims, however, are confused and unsure about what to do, who to tell, and where to go for help.

Rape experts recommend that victims immediately go to a safe place and telephone a local rape crisis center, where counselors are available to offer free, confidential assistance. They can inform teens about which hospitals in their area provide the best services for rape victims, and they can also accompany victims to the emergency room. At the hospital, crisis counselors can make sure treatment guidelines are followed, advise teens about their legal options, and provide

57

emotional support. As rape expert Andrea Parrot points out, by emphasizing that "poor judgment is not a rapeable offense,"[74] and that no one has the right to force sexual activity upon another person, counselors can begin the process of diffusing destructive self-blame.

Teen victims may also want to call a friend or family member to go with them to the hospital for support. If they do not feel ready to tell their parents, they may want to call a close friend, relative, teacher, or any other trusted adult.

The importance of seeking medical assistance

Seeking immediate medical assistance is vital in order to get emergency contraception to prevent pregnancy, as well as to receive evaluation and treatment for sexually transmitted diseases and any physical injuries. While injuries do not always occur, female adolescent victims may suffer from physical trauma to the reproductive or urinary tract, including vaginal bleeding, bruises, lacerations, and contusions. Trauma is apt to be more extensive among younger females and virginal adolescents. Male teen victims also need to be evaluated and treated for sexually transmitted diseases and are more likely to have incurred serious physical injuries.

It is also important to seek medical attention for purposes of collecting evidence and documenting injuries. Victims do not have to decide immediately whether or not they want to press charges. Even if they think they will not pursue legal action, it is a good idea to have medical evidence collected, should they decide to press charges later.

Prior to going to the hospital, rape victims should avoid the strong urge to shower or throw away clothing worn during an assault. Washing, changing clothes, douching, brushing teeth, or even combing one's hair can destroy crucial evidence.

Significant improvements in the treatment of rape victims

In general, the treatment of rape victims has vastly improved and become better coordinated in recent decades. There is a much better understanding about how traumatic rape is and about the importance of providing victims with support. Once a victim calls a rape crisis hot line, arrives at the emergency room, or reports the crime, a multidisciplinary Sexual Assault Response Team, which includes medical, victim services, and law enforcement representatives, is often formed to address his or her physical, psychological, and legal needs.

Before such enlightened treatment programs, rape victims who went to the hospital often spent hours waiting to be examined in crowded, hectic emergency rooms. When they were finally seen, they could not count on knowledgeable and sensitive treatment from medical personnel. With increasing awareness that such an initial hospital experience can further traumatize a victim, the medical community has initiated dramatic improvements. A growing number of hospitals and clinics have added specially trained Sexual Assault Nurse Examiners (SANEs) to the staff who evaluate and treat

Seeking medical assistance immediately after a rape occurs is vital to the victim's health. Immediate reporting also allows authorities to collect evidence concerning the crime.

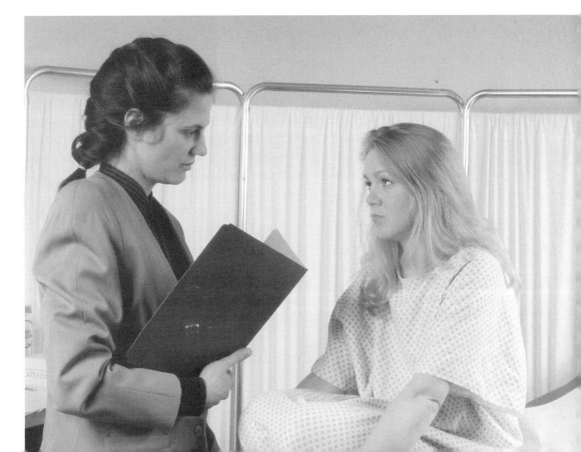

victims, collect and document evidence, and refer victims to follow-up medical care and counseling. Many hospitals now provide a quiet, confidential room separate from the emergency room in which rape victims can be examined.

In some states, medical personnel and other adults are required to notify the police of the rape of a minor who is under the age of eighteen, with or without the victim's consent. Some hospital staff also automatically contact the police whenever a rape victim seeks medical treatment. Even if there is no requirement or policy in place to notify the police, and a victim does not plan to press charges, most victim advocates encourage victims to make a report. Early reporting to the police will make a case stronger, should a victim decide to go to court later. In addition, in most states, reporting an assault to the police makes a victim eligible for victim compensation programs that pay for evidential examinations, testing, treatment, and additional services. It also puts the police and the perpetrator on notice, should the rapist attempt future assaults.

Teenage rape victims today can also expect to receive more respectful and sympathetic treatment from police personnel than was typically the case in the past. Most officers now receive special training about sexual assault. As Daniel Schelbe, chairman of emergency medicine at an Akron, Ohio, hospital, notes: "The feeling used to be, 'I've been physically assaulted, and now I'm going to be assaulted by the medical and legal systems.' I think we've come a long way in helping to ease those concerns."[75]

Even with the best of care and treatment by medical and law enforcement personnel, recovering from rape takes time. In the weeks and months after an assault, the quality of emotional support a victim receives is a major factor in his or her ability to make a successful recovery. A strong support system may include: trusted family members and friends; a counselor or therapist; and a support group.

Support from family and friends

The first person a teen victim often confides in about the rape is a close friend. A friend who offers unconditional love

and support helps a victim begin the healing process. On the other hand, if a friend blames, criticizes, or doubts a victim, the pain of the experience will increase and last longer.

Discussing the crime with supportive friends can help rape survivors to heal.

Rape experts advise communicating the following ideas to a victim: "It was not your fault"; "The rapist is the only one who is to blame"; "I am so glad you are alive"; "I am so sorry this happened to you"; and "You did what you needed to do to survive." Male victims also need reassurance that an assault has nothing to do with their sexual orientation and that they are not alone.

To be discouraged are damaging comments and questions such as: "You are the one to blame"; "Did you do anything to lead him on?"; "You should not have . . ."; "Why didn't you . . . ?"; "Get over it already!"; "I don't believe you"; "Other people have it worse off than you"; and "Do not talk about it."

Talking about their experience is a fundamental way in which victims release their pain and anger and begin working through their grief and distress. One of the most helpful things friends can do is to be available to listen without interrupting, yelling, or injecting their own feelings. Discussions, however, must be on a victim's timetable. Each rape victim recovers in a different way. Some victims may want to talk to friends and trusted family members immediately. Others may turn to loved ones for support later, during the healing process. What matters is that family and friends let victims know that they are available to listen when survivors feel ready to talk.

Loved ones can also be supportive by asking whether victims want to be touched. Many victims, especially within the first few weeks after an assault, prefer to avoid physical contact, even with those whom they love and trust. Friends and family members can help by being patient, giving victims the space they need, and doing their best not to take a victim's physical withdrawal personally.

Teen victims may feel reassured by having a close friend or family member accompany them to appointments.

Of course, if victims indicate that they want the comfort and reassurance of hugs, counselors encourage offering hugs

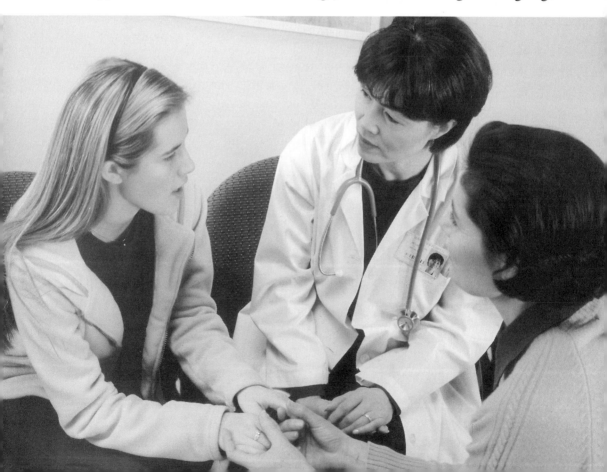

with empathy. Trauma expert Patti Levin points out that hugging can be very therapeutic, prompting the release of endogenous opioids, the body's natural painkillers.

Family and friends can also help victims recover by not trying to take over and make decisions for victims. Rape involves a loss of control and feelings of powerlessness. Respecting victims' rights to make their own decisions about recovery is an important way to help them reclaim a sense of control over their own lives.

By helping seek out resources and exploring treatment and legal options, friends and loved ones can provide practical assistance as well. In addition, they can help a victim by offering to accompany her to treatment and appointments and by being on hand for those times when she expects to encounter a rapist. Many teen victims dread seeing their attacker(s) at school, and the company of trusted friends as they go to and from classes and school activities can be very reassuring.

Sometimes, friends of rape victims feel so angry and upset that they express their desire to exact revenge by attacking the rapist(s). Threatening to take violent action, however, only adds to a victim's anxiety and distress by leading him or her to worry about the safety of friends. Instead, friends can be most helpful when they maintain focus on providing the victim with support.

To do the best job of attending to the needs of victims, family members and friends need to care for themselves. As secondary victims, they too may feel traumatized and violated. In addition to educating themselves about the trauma of rape, family members and friends should not hesitate to seek counseling for themselves if needed.

The importance of therapy

Even the most well-meaning loved ones may push victims to "get over it" before they are ready, or unintentionally make comments that hurt, rather than help, victims. Many rape survivors report that talking to a counselor or therapist gave them relief that they were unable to find anywhere else. Laura Strickland, a rape victim, says: "If I could tell a rape victim only one thing, it would be that the experience leaves a real wound, one that requires professional help. I eventually found my way into a rape-counselor's office. She was a soft-spoken person with a pleasant face and gentle smile. I sat on her couch and talked and cried and healed. She is one of the reasons I'm alive today."[76]

A rape counselor or therapist can provide victims with important information about rape myths and rape trauma syndrome and with reassurance that the painful symptoms they are experiencing are normal reactions to the trauma of rape. A sensitive therapist can offer support in working through anger and grief and can assist victims in developing coping skills. Above all, a therapist can help victims eradicate destructive self-blame. As Cherise explains:

> The most important step in my healing was forgiving myself for what had happened. I realized that I was still blaming myself for the rape. My therapist told me to talk to myself in the mirror, to tell myself that I'm a good person and that I didn't deserve to be hurt. I had to believe that it wasn't my fault, that I didn't need to punish myself for what that man had done to me.[77]

The value of support groups

Rape crisis centers and hospitals frequently offer rape recovery support groups, including groups specifically for teen victims. Many teens think that attending a support group is the last thing they are interested in doing, and then are pleasantly surprised that participating in one helps them feel better and more capable of getting on with their lives. Groups can help break down feelings of isolation, guilt, and self-blame after the rape. The experience of providing support to others in the group can also restore a victim's sense of meaning and purpose.

Jennifer, who was raped by a stranger on her way to the supermarket when she was thirteen, found that attending group meetings contributed significantly to her recovery. She built connections with people who had had similar experiences, she felt less alone, and she also found that she could talk more freely about her experience and pain than she could with her family: "With my family, I felt, Why should I burden them with this thing? Not that *they* felt it was a burden, but to me it was. And I didn't want them to think I was upset all the time."[78]

Self-care activities that aid recovery

Rape experts recommend that recovering teens regularly engage in activities that comfort and nurture them, as well as help them feel stronger and more positive about themselves. For example, many teen victims say that writing about the rape in a journal was helpful to them in working through their pain. Others report that artistic activities such as music, drawing, or dance were healing. Still others say they got some relief from anxiety and stress by taking hot baths, getting massages, or doing yoga.

Many survivors say that prayer and/or meditation helped them recover and that they also found solace in reading books about recovering rape victims. Others report that engaging in strenuous physical activity, such as jogging, aerobics, and bicycling, helped them feel stronger and better about themselves. For some survivors, taking a self-defense class boosted their self-confidence and helped them feel less vulnerable to future assaults.

Self-care activities like yoga and dance can help rape survivors feel comforted, positive, and strong.

Empowerment through taking action

Despite the difficulties of prosecuting rapists, particularly acquaintance rapists, some rape survivors have found that taking their assailants to court was empowering. As Lyndsey explained about her decision to press criminal charges against the two boys who had gotten her drunk and raped her: "At first, I wasn't really sure what had happened and thought maybe it was my fault. But I'm glad that once it sank in that I was raped, I fought to make these guys pay for what they did instead of being ashamed."[79]

Many state laws allow victims to file civil suits against their attackers for pain, suffering, and for therapy and medical costs. Some rape victims choose this legal option instead of, or in addition to, pressing criminal charges because of its greater probability of success. A guilty verdict in a civil suit requires a majority vote by jurors, rather than unanimity. The burden of proof in a civil suit is also somewhat less stringent. There must be a preponderance of evidence indicating guilt, rather than absolute certainty "beyond a reasonable doubt."

In addition to legal action, helping other victims can also be empowering for survivors. For example, date-rape drug victim Tammy Ivar testified before Congress to help pass the Date-Rape Drug Prohibition Act of 2000. This bill made it much harder for rapists who drug victims to get off easily, as her assailant had. Tammy found that the experience was tremendously affirming:

> A group of molestation and incest victims were sitting behind me during the testimony, all between the ages of 12 and 16. Many of them came up to me afterward and said, "Thank you so much for doing this." They looked up to me because I spoke out! I was no longer a rape victim. I was a hero. . . . In the end, what happened to me helped a lot of girls because I wasn't afraid to tell my story. I realized that the only way anyone can create something positive out of rape is to come forward. [80]

Other survivors have found solace in volunteering to work with a rape crisis center or in other prevention programs. After seventeen-year-old Loren was raped by a stranger, she found that making presentations to high school students about how to stay safe from rape helped her recover.

Despite the trauma of rape, victims can and do recover. Some teen rape survivors even say that the experience, as horrible as it was, helped them become stronger and more mature. As trauma expert Patti Levin says: "Hardly anyone would choose to be traumatized as a vehicle for growth. Yet our experience shows that people are incredibly resilient, and the worst traumas and crises can become enabling, empowering transformations." [81]

Unfortunately, however, teenagers are the least likely to make a healthy recovery because most do not seek the help that they need. The vulnerability of teens to rape and its destructive aftermath has led a number of health professionals, victim advocates, and educators to develop programs aimed at adolescent rape intervention and prevention.

6

Intervention and Prevention

BECAUSE TEEN RAPE victims are the least likely to seek help and are at significant risk for being victimized again, rape-prevention experts advocate focusing efforts on identifying and reaching out to already-victimized teens. Increasingly, the medical community is being called upon to help. Health-care providers are in a unique position to identify victims because they are apt to see teenagers in the relatively private setting of a medical office, where they can assure teens of confidentiality.

Both the American Medical Association and the American Academy of Pediatrics strongly recommend that health-care providers routinely screen adolescents for sexual victimization. Screening should take place away from parents, friends, or dating partners. Since more than 70 percent of victims who have had an experience that would legally qualify as rape do not use that term to describe their experience, experts advise avoiding the word "rape." Instead, in a nonjudgmental way, physicians and other clinicians should ask teenagers questions such as: "Have you ever had sex?"; "How old were you the first time?"; "Was that something you wanted to do?"; "Has anyone ever forced you to have sex?"; and "Has anyone ever talked you into having sex when you really did not want to?"[82]

The American Academy of Pediatrics advises pediatricians to be prepared to offer emotional support and appropriate referrals for assistance. Clinicians must become knowledgeable about services in the community for adolescent sexual-assault victims. They also need to be aware of current reporting requirements in their communities, and keep themselves updated about continuing advances in the technology used to examine victims. For example, DNA technology now makes it possible to perform a forensic examination beyond the seventy-two-hour period that was previously considered the cutoff.

Health-care providers must be alert to the relationship of rape and sexual abuse to other problems teens may present. Substance abuse, risky sexual behavior, premature pregnancy, depression, and suicide attempts may be symptoms of victimization. So that they can provide support and make needed referrals, clinicians must try to find out if a history of sexual victimization is an underlying cause of the problems teens present.

Because many teens are unlikely to seek help after a rape, adults, especially health-care providers, must be aware of the signs and symptoms of abuse.

Health-care providers can also play a role in prevention. As the American Academy of Pediatrics points out, "Many adolescents lack the skills necessary to recognize and avoid potentially violent dating situations."[83] Clinicians can provide patients with information about: the difference between healthy and unhealthy, nonconsensual, exploitative relationships; warning signs of potential danger in dating relationships; typical settings for acquaintance or date rape; the dangers of date-rape drugs and late-night use of alcohol and drugs; the importance of clear communication and setting limits for sexual activity ahead of time; and rape resistance strategies.

If health-care providers are to take a much more proactive role in intervention and prevention efforts, they must be prepared. Incorporating victimization issues into medical and nursing school curricula is vital. In addition, as rape expert Holly Harner points out, reinstating funding for school nurses and training them to recognize victimization would significantly increase the ability to identify victims and refer them for help. She recommends that teachers, school counselors, youth workers, and anyone who works regularly with youth also receive specialized training in identifying and providing support to victims.

Redesigning prevention programs

Experts are increasingly recognizing the need to go beyond identifying and assisting victims. Broad-based comprehensive educational programs aimed at all teens must be put in place to prevent rape from happening in the first place.

In the past, prevention programs focused on educating teen and young adult women on how to prevent sexual assault, including avoiding unsafe situations and learning self-defense tactics. The limitations of this approach have become apparent. It perpetuated the myth that victims were responsible for preventing sexual assault. By falsely implying that there were guaranteed ways to stay safe from sexual assault, it stigmatized victims as having "failed" by not stopping their attackers. These programs were also not particularly effective in acquaintance-rape situations.

The current prevailing view among prevention experts is that rape will not be prevented until rapists, most of whom are male, stop raping. Therefore, educational prevention programs must address the attitudes, beliefs, and behaviors of males as well as females. In addition, educational efforts must start early because of the vulnerability of young people to sexual violence. A growing body of research reveals that sexual coercion is a problem for younger adolescents in middle and junior high schools, as well as for older adolescents in high school and college. Educational prevention curricula need to be offered in middle schools, as well as in high schools and colleges.

Content of teen rape prevention programs

Because teen rape, dating violence, and abusive dating relationships are closely interrelated, prevention programs increasingly address these issues together. It has become clear that adolescents of both sexes need accurate information and understanding of the nature of rape, the dangers of abusive dating relationships, and the importance of mutual respect and equality in healthy relationships. Adolescents must be exposed to positive alternatives to sexual violence and abusive relationships. As rape expert Andrea Parrot notes: "Programs that employ scare tactics or point out only what is wrong with students' current behaviors serve to disempower the students. There must be a component to empower them with new behavioral strategies."[84]

Prevention program topics relevant to dating violence include: the difference between healthy and unhealthy dating relationships; warning signs of a potentially abusive dating relationship; and assertive communication skills. Topics specifically addressing rape include: the nature of rape; myths versus facts about rape (including the reality that males and gay and lesbian teens can be victims as well); rape laws; situations and scenarios that put teenagers at risk, and how to avoid them; positive ways to respond to sexually aggressive behavior displayed by others in a teen's presence; the impact of rape on victims; and finally, the importance of seeking help and what to do in case of rape—who to contact, where to go, and what services are available. Prevention program curricula also need to address the context in which rape and dating violence take place, particularly the sex-role stereotyping and inequalities that pervade adolescent culture and society in general.

Promising prevention programs: ongoing and highly interactive

In 2000, the American College of Obstetricians and Gynecologists published a report on prevention programs around the country, in which they identified certain key characteristics of the most promising programs. Not only did they discover that these programs were comprehensive in their handling of subject matter, but they found that promising programs were ongoing and highly interactive. They included problem-solving exercises, group discussion, role playing, peer education, interactive theatrical presentations, and sometimes emotionally powerful presentations by survivors. In contrast, single-session presentations, especially those in a lecture format, were notably ineffective in changing attitudes or behavior.

Even promising, multi-session programs, however, appeared to have a limited effectiveness in changing behavior. For example, researchers studied the impact of a ten-session dating-violence prevention program called Safe Dates on fifteen hundred eighth and ninth graders in North Carolina. The program was highly interactive and enthusiastically received. It included theater productions performed by peers and poster contests, as well as community activities, such as learning about crisis lines, support groups, and victim services available to adolescents.

One month after the program, its impact seemed to be dramatic. There was a 60 percent reduction in sexual violence, in addition to significant positive changes in attitudes and knowledge about dating violence, gender stereotyping, and awareness of services. However, in a one-year follow-up, while there was still some evidence of positive changes in dating-violence norms and awareness of community services, the short-term impact on behavior had disappeared.

The reduction in sexual violence among the students had disappeared.

Clearly, much more research needs to be done on how to maximize the effectiveness of prevention programs. Based on the research thus far, it appears that to be genuinely effective, programs must be long-term and continue throughout students' secondary school and college experiences. Beginning in middle school, prevention information must be presented as a regular part of student orientations, sexuality education, and health course curricula. In addition, the topics of rape and dating violence should be integrated into the teaching of academic subjects such as literature, social studies, and psychology. Under the auspices of the Wellesley College Center for Research on Women, Nan Stein, for example, has developed a curriculum called Gender Violence/Gender Justice. It features works of literature (*I Know Why the Caged Bird Sings* by Maya Angelou) and works of contemporary history (*Our Guys: The Glen Ridge Rape and the Secret Life of the Perfect Suburb* by Bernard Lefkowitz) that can be used in lesson plans dealing with rape.

The importance of involving teens and other community experts

Prevention programs are much more likely to be relevant and effective if local teens are involved in planning and presenting them. Teens are likely to be the best informed about the issues and pressures facing young people in their community and can help ensure that presentations are adapted to their peers' real-life concerns and experiences. In tailoring programs that are appropriate for groups of varying ages, racial and cultural backgrounds, and sexual orientation—the input of young people is invaluable as well. In addition, teenagers who attend prevention programs are much less likely to dismiss information presented by their peers than they are from adult authority figures.

Experts also recommend that entire communities become involved in efforts to educate teens about sexual-assault issues, and they advise schools to collaborate with other community groups, youth advocates, and rape awareness experts

in developing prevention programming. Possibilities include: staff from the rape crisis centers; former rape victims; sex-offender treatment providers; youth organizations such as boys' and girls' clubs and church youth groups; health-care providers; advocates for teens with disabilities; law enforcement personnel; public-policy makers; and university faculty, researchers, and students. Getting parents involved and providing them with resources on how to talk with their teens about rape and dating violence also contribute to the effectiveness of prevention programs.

Rape prevention programs like this one involving group discussions and peer interaction have a higher success rate than programs organized around a lecture format.

In their article "The Healthy Relationships Program: Preventing Sexual Assault of Youth," Victoria Lutzer and Norma Day-Vines present a case study of a high school collaboration with other community groups. The school's health-care team worked with a local battered-women's shelter, along with a performing group and community psychology interns from the local university, to develop and implement an interactive program aimed both at special and regular education students. Following sexual-assault prevention presentations, students were given the option of signing up for eight weeks of small-group counseling sessions. Because most of those who signed up were already involved in abusive relationships, staff from the local domestic violence shelter took over leading the groups. At the conclusion of the eight-week sessions, participants requested that the groups continue, and several students attended them throughout their four years in high school.

Preparing for disclosure

Experts agree that it is vital to have a counselor on hand to provide necessary support to teens who may disclose being rape or dating-violence victims as a result of participating in a prevention program. In the Brooklyn, New York–based Victim Services' Safe Harbor program, schools create a "Safe Harbor Room." During and following sexual-assault prevention programs, the room serves as a safe place where teens can disclose their victimization, receive emotional support, and get referrals for additional counseling and victim services.

As Andrea Parrot points out, one of the valuable consequences of prevention programs is that victims who may have previously rejected the idea of getting help may come forward. If they decide to get follow-up counseling, they have a much better chance of making a healthy emotional recovery.

Making prevention programs male-friendly

While most rapists are male, most males do not rape and can also be victims as well. Prevention programs that appear to bash males and ignore male victimization may create a backlash among teen males. According to male-rape expert Frederick Mathews: "It is not uncommon to hear male students express resentment toward high school anti-violence curricula that presumes them to be abusers, harassers, rapists, and sexual assaulters in waiting. Indeed, it is difficult to feel part of a collective social movement against violence when one's own experiences are dismissed, excluded or minimized."[85]

To increase effectiveness of programming, prevention experts recommend that males actively participate. According to researchers Patricia D. Rozee, Py Bateman, and Theresa Gilmore, "Experiential exercises requiring males to draw upon their own lifestyle, experiences, and knowledge are particularly effective in eliciting attitude change."[86]

Experts often recommend that programs specifically targeted at males be presented by highly respected males, such as student leaders, sports team captains, and college and professional athletes. As Parrot says: "If professional athletes can sell after-shave lotion and socks, should they not be able to sell the concept of respect for women?"[87]

Outstanding organizations that provide programs targeting male adolescents include Men Can Stop Rape and Men Overcoming Violence. Men Can Stop Rape is a Washington, D.C.–based group dedicated to supporting young males in challenging the "rape culture" in which they live. Active both locally and nationally, the group offers a number of prevention programs for young men in middle school, high school, and college. Their programs are designed to challenge preexisting attitudes about the impact of violence on both males and females, assist young men in redefining masculinity, and encourage males to take an active role in preventing violence in their communities.

Men Overcoming Violence (MOVE) is a San Francisco–based group which offers the MOVE Youth program, dedicated to ending young men's violence and abuse in their relationships. MOVE includes teen dating-violence prevention programs throughout the San Francisco Unified School District, as well as high school peer educator training (teens counseling teens), support groups for male teens, weekly workshops for incarcerated youth, and counseling services for teen men who have been sexually or physically violent in their relationships. In addition, they offer professional training to community agencies and schools.

Male and female activists participate in an antiviolence rally. Such rallies try to encourage people to take active roles in preventing violence in their communities.

The work that MOVE does with incarcerated youth and violent male teens is a good example of programming that targets high-risk groups. Another example is the Youth Relationships Project, a program aimed at self-awareness and social change. In this eighteen-session community program, teens from abusive backgrounds first learn about dating violence and examine their own lives and experiences. The program then encourages them to become involved in working for change within their peer groups, the teen culture, and the broader community. In their two-year follow-up research on its impact, David Wolfe and Peter Jaffe report that there has been a significant decrease in participants' violent behavior toward dating partners.

Changing school and community culture

As the American College of Obstetricians and Gyne-cologists notes in *Drawing the Line,* the nation's schools and communities should reflect a commitment to zero tolerance for sexism, rape, and harassment. Teens are likely to ignore efforts to influence their attitudes and behaviors if they per-ceive that adults do not "practice what they preach" and do not take sexual violence seriously.

All teachers and staff members in schools must receive ongoing teacher training and educational support on sexism and rape. Administrators must take a strong stand against rape, sexual assault, and harassment. Rules outlawing harass-ment and sexual assault must be in place and stringently enforced.

As Parrot points out, the way in which school adminis-trators deal with acquaintance-rape cases determines the extent to which future cases are reported and the chances of a reduction in the number of rapes. The eruption of a major scandal at the nation's Air Force Academy provides a good example of the problems that can ensue when an institution fails to take a strong stand against sexual assault. In 2003, five former female cadets came forward and reported that when they had complained to academy officials about being raped, they were faced with indifference, inaction, and blame. Instead of holding the attackers accountable, officials blamed the young women and punished them for infractions such as drinking and socializing with upperclassmen.

Despite the existence of a rape crisis line and academy rules forbidding sexual assault, the officials' response to these five women was apparently not unusual. Another cadet who had been raped at the academy, and subsequently left in 2001, said: "I probably knew 100 women when I was at the Air Force Academy. I would say 80 experienced a sex-ual assault, and probably 40 of them were rape."[88] Yet anoth-er young woman said that a health counselor at the academy told a group of female cadets that if they reported a rape and asked for an investigation, "your entire life at the academy is over, and you'll probably get kicked out."[89]

Fortunately, the scandal that erupted resulted in an independent investigation, an administrative shake-up, and a commitment to making major changes in the academy's policies and overall culture. The academy's ability to attract female cadets and recover from its tarnished reputation will depend upon its making it clear that rape, sexual assault, and sexism will no longer be tolerated.

To prevent rape, changing the culture of the wider community is vital as well. Clergy, youth workers, politicians, and other community leaders must take a strong stand and speak out against sexual violence. Policy makers and lawmakers must continue to monitor and strengthen laws against rape and ensure that they are enforced. Victim advocates must continue to reach out to youth in the community in a variety of settings, including school-based health centers, malls, athletic centers, youth groups, temples, and churches. Services for adolescent victims must be expanded and improved. An encouraging development is the creation of the Teen Victim Project. The project is a joint effort of the National Center for Victims of Crime and the National Council on Crime and Delinquency aimed at raising awareness about the impact of crimes against teenagers, and creating a national network of service providers to meet the needs of victimized teens.

The strategic role of parents in preventing teen rape

Research indicates that parents are the most influential role models in their children's lives. Parents who consistently model mutual respect, loving support, and equality in their intimate relationships, can greatly increase the probabilities that their teenagers will gravitate toward healthy relationships and avoid becoming involved in violent dating relationships.

It is also critically important for parents to support their teens' self-esteem, maintain open communication about sex and relationships, and actively listen to their teenagers' concerns. A major problem for many teens victimized by rape and dating violence is the lack of trusted adults in their lives

Parents are crucial to a teenager's development. Teens who are part of loving, supportive families have a better chance of developing healthy dating relationships.

whom they feel they can turn to for emotional support and help.

In *I Never Called It Rape,* Robin Warshaw stresses the importance of parents speaking with their children about sexual rights and responsibilities, starting at an early age. As children move into adolescence, parents must talk about rape, the dangers of drinking and drugs, and the many choices and pressures they will encounter. Parents should also push for prevention programming in their teenagers' schools and youth groups.

Joe Kelly, the founder of *New Moon* magazine and the author of *Dads and Daughters,* also stresses the importance of parents helping their teens become more aware of the destructive and inaccurate media portrayal of girls and women as sex objects. He advises parents to watch, read, and listen to media with their teens, talk over what they observe, and complain to advertisers and entertainment providers when the messages are negative and destructive. In discussing music videos that reinforce the idea that a girl's primary purpose is to provide males with sexual pleasure, Kelly comments: "If you are silent about the things your kids hear from media and culture, then those things gain an authority that they do not deserve."[90]

Well-adjusted teenagers like these often grow up with parents who encourage self-esteem, talk openly about sex, and listen to their teens' concerns.

The big picture

Clearly, teenagers need the support and caring of trusted adults to help them stay safe from rape. Numerous experts also maintain, however, that the problem of rape will never be eliminated until there is no longer an imbalance of power between men and women, which means effecting fundamental social and cultural changes. Others further argue the need for systematic efforts to challenge the glorification of violence and the linking of sex to violence that pervades the wider culture.

This is a tall order and will not happen overnight. Yet, every individual and group dedicated to working toward gender equality at home, in schools, and in the workplace is steering society toward the elimination of rape and sexual violence. Each person who works for positive, nonsexist, nonviolent images in the media is helping America become a less rape-prone society. Every caring adult who models and teaches teens about healthy relationships, and who reaches out to build caring relationships with teenagers, is contributing to the elimination of teen rape. Each teen who resists being a passive bystander and takes a stand against the rape and abuse of peers is contributing to a reduction in teen rape. In short, everyone can make a difference in helping to create a society in which rape and its destructive aftermath no longer threaten the well-being of teenagers.

Notes

Chapter 1: Teenagers Are Especially Vulnerable to Rape

1. National Victim Center and the Crime Victims Research and Treatment Center, *Rape in America: A Report to the Nation,* pamphlet, April 23, 1992, p. 15.

2. Interview by author, Louisville, KY, December 21, 2001. All interviews were conducted in confidentiality, and names are changed in text to protect individuals' privacy.

3. Dean G. Kilpatrick, "Rape and Sexual Assault," National Violence Against Women Prevention Research Center, 2000. www.vawprevention.org.

4. Kilpatrick, "Rape and Sexual Assault."

5. Quoted in Alison Bell, "Date Rape," *Teen Magazine,* July 1997.

6. National Sexual Violence Resource Center, "One in Five Teenage Girls Experiences Dating Violence," 2001. www.nsvrc.org.

7. Salina Stone, "They Said I Was 'Young and Immature,'" in *Dating Violence: Young Women in Danger,* ed. Barrie Levy. Seattle, WA: Seal, 1998, p. 29.

8. Nancy Worcester, "A More Hidden Crime: Adolescent Battered Women," *Network News,* July–August 1993.

9. Elizabeth, "'Dating' Is a Heterosexual Concept," *Dating Violence,* 1998, p. 42.

10. Quoted in Maria Alvarez, "I Waited 11 Years to Nail My Rapist," *Cosmopolitan,* November 1997.

11. Quoted in Bell, "Date Rape."

12. Quoted in Laura Gilbert, "Danger: The Risk of Being a Teenage Girl," *Teen Magazine,* June 2001.

13. Quoted in Michael W. Lynch, "Enforcing 'Statutory Rape'?" *Public Interest,* Summer 1998.

14. Quoted in Lloyd Gite, "When Boys Are Raped," *Essence,* November 1991.

15. Quoted in Aurora Mackey, "Sexual Hazards: Protecting Yourself and Your Body," *Teen Magazine,* February 1984.

16. Quoted in *Teen Magazine,* "Rape: The Scary Reality," November 1994.

17. Quoted in Michelle Stacey, "Bad Boys," *Seventeen,* November 1993, p. 126.

18. Quoted in Mimi Swartz, "Brenham's Paradise Lost," *Texas Monthly,* February 1997.

Chapter 2: The Causes of Rape

19. Martin D. Schwartz and Walter S. DeKeseredy, *Sexual Assault on the College Campus.* Thousand Oaks, CA: Sage, 1997, p. 47.

20. Quoted in Maggie Fox, "Hour of TV a Day Leads to Violence, Study Finds," Children Now, March 28, 2002. www.childrennow.org.

21. Quoted in Fox, "Hour of TV a Day Leads to Violence."

22. Quoted in Anastasia Toufexis, "Teenagers and Sex Crimes: A New Jersey Assault Dramatizes the Rise in Offenses by Youths," *Time,* June 5, 1989, p. 60.

23. Quoted in Bill Hewitt, "The Body Counters (High School Students Track Their Sexual Activities)," *People Weekly,* April 12, 1993.

24. Ruth Kershner, "Adolescent Attitudes About Rape," *Adolescence,* Spring 1996.

25. Jeanne Boxley, Lynette Lawrance, and Harvey Gruchow, "A Preliminary Study of Eighth Grade Students' Attitudes Toward Rape Myths and Women's Roles," *Journal of School Health,* March 1995.

26. Quoted in Lynn Phillips, *The Girls Report: What We Know and Need to Know About Growing Up Female.* New York: National Council for Research on Women, 1998, p. 50.

27. Quoted in Robin Warshaw, *I Never Called It Rape*. New York: HarperPerennial, 1994, p. 40.

28. Robin Warshaw and Andrea Parrot, "The Contribution of Sex-Role Socialization to Acquaintance Rape," in *Acquaintance Rape: The Hidden Crime*, eds., Andrea Parrot and Laurie Bechhofer. New York: John Wiley and Sons, 1991, p. 74.

29. Schwartz and DeKeseredy, *Sexual Assault on the College Campus*, p. 47.

30. Warshaw, *I Never Called It Rape*, p. 120.

31. Quoted in Bill Hewitt, "The Body Counters."

32. Quoted in Beth Weinhouse, "Young but Not Innocent: A Shocking Report on Kids Who Rape," *Redbook*, April 1990, p. 137.

33. Mary Pipher, *Reviving Ophelia: Saving the Selves of Adolescent Girls*. New York: Ballantine, 1994, p. 207.

34. Jill Murray, *But I Love Him*. New York: HarperCollins, 2000, p. 2.

35. Interview by author, Louisville, KY, December 21, 2001.

36. Nancy Worcester, "A More Hidden Crime."

37. Quoted in Suzanne Fields, "Rape as Sport: The Culture Is the Root," *Insight on the News*, May 3, 1993.

Chapter 3: Risk Factors for Rape

38. Quoted in Richard J. Sagall, "Sex Abuse and Teen Pregnancy," *Pediatrics for Parents*, June 1988, p. 7.

39. Pipher, *Reviving Ophelia*, p. 229.

40. Quoted in Weinhouse, "Young but Not Innocent," p. 138.

41. Debbie Mattson, "Belonging," in *Dating Violence*, p. 35.

42. Stacey, "Bad Boys," p. 127.

43. Murray, *But I Love Him*, p. 72.

44. Jan K. Jenson, "If Only . . . ," in *Dating Violence*, p. 47.

45. Murray, *But I Love Him*, p. 75.

46. Interview by author, Louisville, KY, June 27, 2003.

47. Quoted in Richard Demak, "Athletes and Rape," *Sports Illustrated*, March 23, 1992, p. 7.

48. Schwartz and DeKeseredy, *Sexual Assault on the College Campus,* p. 107.

49. Quoted in Anastasia Toufexis, "Sex and the Sporting Life: Do Athletic Teams Unwittingly Promote Assaults and Rape?" *Time,* August 6, 1990.

50. Quoted in Amy Cunningham, "Sex in High School: What's Love Got to Do with It?" *Glamour,* September 1993, p. 319.

51. Interview by author, Lexington, KY, June 27, 2003.

52. Interview by author, Lexington, KY, June 25, 1998.

53. Quoted in Elizabeth Karlsberg, "Acquaintance Rape: What You Should Know," *Teen Magazine,* November 1991, p. 14.

Chapter 4: The Impact of Rape

54. Barry R. Burkhart, "Conceptual and Practical Analysis of Therapy for Acquaintance Rape Victims," in *Acquaintance Rape,* p. 291.

55. Quoted in Karlsberg, "Aquaintance Rape," p. 16.

56. Interview by author, Lexington, KY, June 25, 1998.

57. Stephen A. Schmidt, "To Speak of Rape: A Father's Experience," *Christian Century,* January 6, 1993.

58. Rebecca Campbell, "Mental Health Services for Rape Survivors: Current Issues in Therapeutic Practice," October 2001. www.vaw.umn.edu.

59. Quoted in Doria Biddle, "Skin Deep, a Story of Secret Cutting," *Teen Magazine,* January 2001.

60. Quoted in Kimberly Coniff Taber, "I Was at a Party," *CosmoGirl!* June 2002.

61. Alvarez, "I Waited 11 Years to Nail My Rapist."

62. Me Ra Koh, "My Boyfriend Raped Me," *Campus Life,* September 2001.

63. Me Ra Koh, "My Boyfriend Raped Me."

64. Quoted in Warshaw, *I Never Called It Rape,* p. 68.

65. Quoted in Taber, "I Was at a Party."

66. Quoted in Alison Bell, "I Was Raped!," *Teen Magazine,* November 1992.

67. *Voices of Rape,* Rev. ed. New York: Franklin Watts, 1998, pp. 52–53.

68. Quoted in Alvarez. "I Waited 11 Years to Nail My Rapist."

69. Quoted in Charlotte Pierce-Baker, *Surviving the Silence, Black Women's Stories of Rape.* New York: W.W. Norton, 1998, p. 149.

70. Quoted in Biddle, "Skin Deep."

71. Quoted in Biddle, "Skin Deep."

72. Quoted in Bell, "I Was Raped!"

Chapter 5: Recovering from Rape

73. Quoted in Bell, "I Was Raped!"

74. Andrea Parrot, "Medical Community Responds to Aquaintance Rape Recommendations," in *Acquaintance Rape, the Hidden Crime,* p. 312.

75. Quoted in Scott Suttell, "Care of Rape Victims Takes SANE Approach," *Crain's Cleveland Business,* October 6, 1997.

76. Laura Strickland, "Healing in Helping: A Rape-Victim's Story of Recovery," *Psychology Today,* March/April 2002, p. 61.

77. Quoted in Biddle, "Skin Deep."

78. Quoted in Pierce-Baker, *Surviving the Silence,* p. 203.

79. Quoted in Taber, "I Was at a Party."

80. Quoted in Sandy Fertman, "Drugged and Raped," *Teen Magazine,* June 2001, p. 62.

81. Patti Levin, "The Trauma Response," VAWnet Library, 1989. www.vawnet.org.

Chapter 6: Intervention and Prevention

82. Deborah Kaplan and Melisa M. Holmes, "Clinical Management of Rape in Adolescent Girls," *Patient Care,* April 30, 1999.

83. "American Academy of Pediatrics, Committee on Adolescence, "Care of the Adolescent Sexual Assault Victim," Pediatrics, June 2001, p. 1476.

84. Andrea Parrot, "Institutional Response: How Can Acquaintance Rape Be Prevented?" in *Acquaintance Rape,* p. 365.

85. Frederick Mathews, "The Invisible Boy: Revisioning the Victimization of Male Children and Teens," National Clearinghouse on Family Violence of Health Canada, 1996 www.hc-sc.gc.ca.

86. Patricia D. Rozee, Py Bateman, and Theresa Gilmore, "The Personal Perspective of Acquaintance Rape Prevention: A Three-Tier Approach," in *Acquaintance Rape,* p. 341.

87. Andrea Parrot, "Institutional Response," p. 362.

88. Quoted in Michael Janofsky, "Air Force Begins an Inquiry of Ex-cadets' Rape Charges," *New York Times,* February 20, 2003. www.nytimes.com.

89. Quoted in Janofsky, "Air Force Begins an Inquiry of Ex-cadets' Rape Charges."

90. Joe Kelly, *Dads and Daughters.* New York: Broadway, 2002, p. 83.

Organizations to Contact

If you need immediate assistance, contact your local rape crisis center (local yellow pages should have listings under Rape Crisis Centers or Human Services), or call one of these two hotlines:

The National Sexual Assault Hotline: 1-800-656-HOPE
The National Domestic Violence Hotline: 1-800-799-SAFE or 1-800-787-3224 (TDD)

For additional information and resources, contact the following organizations:

Center for the Prevention of Sexual and Domestic Violence (CPSDV)
2400 N. 45th St., # 10
Seattle, WA 98103
(206) 634-1903
www.cpsdv.org

CPSDV is an interreligious nonprofit organization dedicated to providing religious leaders and other human-services professionals with education and prevention resources about sexual and domestic violence. The organization produces videos and publications specifically geared to teens and sexual violence.

Men Can Stop Rape Now (MCSR)
PO Box 57144
Washington, DC 20037
(202) 265-6530
www.mencanstoprape.org

MCSR is a nonprofit organization that grew out of D.C. Men Against Rape, a group organized to raise consciousness about men's violence against women. Created in 1997, MCSR offers a variety of educational resources and programming and has worked with young people and youth-serving professionals around the country to engage young men in preventing men's violence.

Rape, Abuse & Incest National Network (RAINN)
635-B Pennsylvania Ave. SE
Washington, DC 20003
(202) 544-1034
(800) 656-4673
www.rainn.org

RAINN is the nation's largest anti–sexual assault organization. It operates the National Sexual Assault Hotline, which offers free, confidential services. The organization is also dedicated to educating the public about sexual assault as well as advocating for improvements in services to victims and for the prosecution of rapists.

U.S. Department of Justice Office on Violence Against Women
810 Seventh St. NW
Washington, DC 20531
(202) 307-6026
www.ojp.usdoj.gov

Created in 1995, the Office on Violence Against Women provides leadership in the federal government's role in addressing violence against women. It provides information about sexual assault, monitors the implementation of legislation, and oversees grant programs to states and territories to establish specialized domestic violence and sexual assault units, assist victims of violence, and hold perpetrators accountable.

For Further Reading

Books

Alexandra Bandon, *Update: Date Rape.* New York: Crestwood House, Macmillan, 1993. An overview of date rape, ways to avoid it, and what to do if you are a victim.

Janet Bode, *Voices of Rape.* Rev. ed. New York: Franklin Watts, 1998. Written for teenagers, *Voices of Rape* provides an overview of the experience of rape and its aftermath, using first-person accounts both of rapists and survivors.

Donna Chaiet, *Staying Safe on Dates.* New York: Rosen, 1995. Advice on how to set clear boundaries in dating situations and deal with sexual assault and rape.

JoAnn Bren Guernsey, *The Facts About Rape.* New York: Crestwood House, Macmillan, 1990. Describes experiences of rape victims and discusses causes of rape, recovery, and prevention.

Laura Kaminker, *Everything You Need to Know About Dealing with Sexual Assault.* New York: Rosen, 1998. Discusses myths and facts about sexual assault and rape, the consequences, recovery, and prevention.

Elaine Landau, *Teenage Violence.* Englewood Cliffs, NJ: Simon and Schuster, 1990. Overview of types of teenage violence, including gang rape and date and acquaintance rape. Also examines the juvenile justice system.

John J. La Valle, *Everything You Need to Know About Being a Male Survivor of Rape or Sexual Assault.* New York: Rosen, 1996. Overview of male rape, especially of children and teenagers, with emphasis on recovery and prevention.

Susan Mufson and Rachel Kranz, *Straight Talk About Date Rape.* New York: Facts On File, 1993. Overview of date and acquaintance rape, why and where they happen, how to avoid being a victim, and where to go for help if you have been victimized.

Andrea Parrot, *Coping with Date Rape and Acquaintance Rape.* New York: Rosen, 1993. Overview of date rape and acquaintance rape: definitions, causes, aftermath, and prevention.

Marvin Rosen, *Dealing with the Effects of Rape and Incest.* Philadelphia: Chelsea House, 2002. Overview of psychological impact of rape and incest on children and teenagers; recovery; and prevention.

Herma Silverstein, *Date Abuse.* Berkeley Heights, NJ: Enslow, 1994. Examines both physical and sexual abuse in dating relationships. Includes discussion of causes, signs, and what to do if you suspect abuse.

Kathleen Winkler, *Date Rape: A Hot Issue.* Berkeley Heights, NJ: Enslow, 1999. Good overview of date or acquaintance rape, the consequences, prevention, and what to do if assaulted.

Websites
Love Is Not Abuse (www.loveisnotabuse.com). Sponsored by Liz Claiborne, this teen-friendly website offers facts, guidance, and resources about abusive teen dating relationships.

TeensHealth (www.kidshealth.org). Created by the Nemours Foundation's Center for Children's Health Media in 1995, TeensHealth and KidsHealth provide teens and families with accurate, up-to-date information on health, relationships, and growing up. The site provides useful information on rape and dating violence.

Works Consulted

Books
E. Sandra Byers and Lucia F. O'Sullivan, eds., *Sexual Coercion in Dating Relationships.* New York: Haworth, 1996. Collection of scholarly articles presenting research and theory on sexual coercion in dating relationships.

Jacqueline Goodchilds et al., "Adolescents and the Perceptions of Sexual Interactions Outcomes." In *Sexual Assault.* Vol. 2, ed. A.W. Burgess. New York: Garland, 1988. A landmark study on adolescent attitudes toward sex, which indicated that most teenagers think forced sex is appropriate under certain circumstances.

Joe Kelly, *Dads and Daughters.* New York: Broadway, 2002. Parenting advice for fathers who want to combat negative cultural images of girls and raise confident, assertive daughters.

Bernard Lefkowitz, *Our Guys: The Glen Ridge Rape and the Secret Life of the Perfect Suburb.* New York: Vintage Books, Random House, 1997. An in-depth study of the gang rape of a mentally retarded girl by a group of popular teenage male athletes. Lefkowitz links America's jock culture to the community's seeming willingness to tolerate adolescent sexual violence against young women.

Barrie Levy, ed., *Dating Violence: Young Women in Danger.* Seattle, WA: Seal, 1998. Experts present a variety of perspectives on adolescent dating violence. Includes personal experiences and discussion of causes, intervention, education, and prevention.

Jill Murray, *But I Love Him.* New York: HarperCollins, 2000. A book of support for parents whose adolescent daughters are in abusive relationships with boyfriends. Includes incisive analysis of why teenage females are vulnerable to sexual and physical abuse in intimate relationships.

Susan Smith Nash, *Dealing with Date Rape: True Stories from Survivors.* Norman, OK: Texture, 1996. Personal experiences of date and acquaintance rape survivors and their challenging journeys toward recovery.

Andrea Parrot and Laurie Bechhofer, eds., *Acquaintance Rape: The Hidden Crime.* New York: John Wiley and Sons, 1991. A variety of experts discuss issues surrounding acquaintance rape: definition, attitudes, myths, causes, types, victims, assailants, societal responses, and avoidance and prevention.

Lynn Phillips, *The Girls Report: What We Know and Need to Know About Growing Up Female.* New York: National Council for Research on Women, 1998. A review and analysis of research and policy studies on adolescent girls in the preceding decade. Includes examination of research on adolescent girls' sexuality and sexual victimization.

Charlotte Pierce-Baker, *Surviving the Silence: Black Women's Stories of Rape.* New York: W.W. Norton, 1998. Author shares her personal experience with being raped and stories of other black women rape survivors.

Mary Pipher, *Reviving Ophelia: Saving the Selves of Adolescent Girls.* New York: Ballantine, 1994. A therapist examines the formidable challenges of growing up female and how caring adults can help girls during the challenging adolescent years. Includes a chapter titled "Sex and Violence."

Martin D. Schwartz and Walter S. DeKeseredy, *Sexual Assault on the College Campus.* Thousand Oaks, CA: Sage, 1997. Sociological examination of sexual assault on college campuses and the role of male peer support in encouraging assaults against women. Good discussion of ways in which culture and gender-role expectations objectify women and increase the likelihood of sexual violence against them.

Robin Warshaw, *I Never Called It Rape.* New York: HarperPerennial, 1994. Updated edition of the *Ms.* Report on

Recognizing, Fighting, and Surviving Date and Acquaintance Rape. The report was based on a survey of more than six thousand college students.

Sheila Weller, *Saint of Circumstance: The Untold Story Behind the Alex Kelly Rape Case: Growing Up Rich and Out of Control.* New York: Pocket Books, Simon and Schuster, 1997. An in-depth look at a brutal rape of a sixteen year old by a star wrestler and ways in which values in a privileged community contributed to a widespread problem of youth violence.

Periodicals

Melissa Abramovitz, "The Knockout Punch of Date Rape Drugs," *Current Health 2: A Weekly Reader Publication,* March 2001.

Lesley Alderman, "Teens: How They Become Victims," *Family PC,* February 2001.

Maria Alvarez, "I Waited 11 Years to Nail My Rapist," *Cosmopolitan,* November 1997.

American Academy of Pediatrics, Committee on Adolescence, "Care of the Adolescent Sexual Assault Victim," *Pediatrics,* June 2001.

————, "Sexual Assault and the Adolescent," *Pediatrics,* November 1994.

American Family Physician, "Risk of Suicide and Past History of Sexual Assault," October 1996.

Karl E. Bauman et al., "An Evaluation of Safe Dates, an Adolescent Dating Violence Prevention Program," *American Journal of Public Health,* January 1998.

Arnold Beichman, "Statutory Rape Laws Must Be Enforced," *Insight on the News,* May 13, 1996.

Alison Bell, "Date Rape," *Teen Magazine,* July 1997.

————, "I Was Raped!" *Teen Magazine,* November 1992.

Doria Biddle, "Skin Deep, a Story of Secret Cutting," *Teen Magazine,* January 2001.

Cheryl Ann Black and Richard R. DeBlassie, "Sexual Abuse in Male Children and Adolescents: Indicators, Effects, and Treatments," *Adolescence,* Spring 1993.

Stephanie Booth, "I Was Raped," *Teen Magazine,* October 1998.

Jeanne Boxley, Lynette Lawrance, and Harvey Gruchow, "A Preliminary Study of Eighth Grade Students' Attitudes Toward Rape Myths and Women's Roles," *Journal of School Health,* March 1995.

Linda Cassidy and Rose Marie Hurrell, "The Influence of Victim's Attire on Adolescents' Judgements of Date Rape," *Adolescence,* Summer 1995.

Amy Cunningham, "Sex in High School: What's Love Got to Do with It?" *Glamour,* September 1993.

Richard Demak, "Athletes and Rape," *Sports Illustrated,* March 23, 1992.

Amy Dickinson, "When Dating Is Dangerous: One in Five Teenage Girls Reports Being a Victim of Violence by Her Date. What Can Parents Do?" *Time,* August 27, 2001.

Mary Buhl Dutta, "Taming the Victim: Rape in Soap Opera," *Journal of Popular Film and Television,* Spring 1999.

M. Jocelyn Elders and Alexa E. Albert, "Adolescent Pregnancy and Sexual Abuse," *JAMA,* August 19, 1998.

Kevin J. Epps, Rebecca Haworth, and Tracey Swaffer, "Attitudes Toward Women and Rape Among Male Adolescents Convicted of Sexual Versus Nonsexual Crimes," *Journal of Psychology,* September 1993.

Sandy Fertman, "Drugged and Raped," *Teen Magazine,* June 2001.

Suzanne Fields, "Rape as Sport: The Culture Is the Root," *Insight on the News,* May 3, 1993.

Robert Finn, "Paralysis Common among Sexual Assault Victims," *Family Practice News,* March 1, 2003.

Vangie A. Foshee et al., "The Safe Dates Program: 1-Year Follow-up Results," *American Journal of Public Health,* October 2000.

David Gelman and Jean Seligmann, "Mixed Messages: California's 'Spur Posse' Scandal Underscores the Varying Signals Society Sends Teens About Sex," *Newsweek,* April 12, 1993.

Nancy Gibbs, "When Is It Rape?" *Time,* June 3, 1991.

C.A. Gidycz et al., "An Evaluation of an Acquaintance Rape Prevention Program: Impact on Attitudes, Sexual Aggression, and Sexual Victimization," *Journal of Interpersonal Violence,* November 2001.

Laura Gilbert, "Danger: The Risk of Being a Teenage Girl," *Teen Magazine,* June 2001.

Lloyd Gite, "When Boys Are Raped," *Essence,* November 1991.

Karen S. Hayward and Dale Elizabeth Pehrsson, "Interdisciplinary Action Supporting Sexual Assault Prevention Efforts in Rural Elementary Schools," *Journal of Community Health Nursing,* Fall 2000.

Bill Hewitt, "The Body Counters (High School Students Track Their Sexual Activities)," *People Weekly,* April 12, 1993.

William H. James et al., "Youth Dating Violence," *Adolescence,* Fall 2000.

Linda Kalof, "Ethnic Differences in Female Sexual Victimization," *Sexuality and Culture,* Fall 2000.

Deborah Kaplan and Melisa M. Holmes, "Clinical Management of Rape in Adolescent Girls," *Patient Care,* April 30, 1999.

Elizabeth Karlsberg, "Acquaintance Rape: What You Should Know," *Teen Magazine,* November 1991.

Ruth Kershner, "Adolescent Attitudes About Rape," *Adolescence,* Spring 1996.

Me Ra Koh, "My Boyfriend Raped Me," *Campus Life,* September 2001.

Joyce F. Lakey, "The Profile and Treatment of Male Adolescent Sex Offenders," *Adolescence,* Winter 1994.

Victoria D. Lutzer and Norma Day-Vines, "The Healthy Relationships Program: Preventing Sexual Assault of Youth," *Reclaiming Children and Youth,* Fall 2001.

Michael W. Lynch, "Enforcing 'Statutory Rape'?" *Public Interest,* Summer 1998.

Aurora Mackey, "Sexual Hazards: Protecting Yourself and Your Body," *Teen Magazine,* February 1984.

Nancy Matsumoto, "Silent Victims," *People Weekly,* June 29, 1992.

Paul McCarthy, "Rape: The Macho View," *Psychology Today,* April 1987.

Judy Monroe, "'Roofies': Horror Drug of the '90s," *Current Health 2: A Weekly Reader Publication,* September 1997.

National Victim Center and the Crime Victims Research and Treatment Center, *Rape in America: A Report to the Nation,* pamphlet, April 23, 1992.

Suzanne O'Malley, "The New Reason Rapists Are Going Free," *Redbook,* August 1997.

People Weekly, "Scoring Points Privately: The Notorious Spur Posse Boys Continue to Date—and Talk," December 27, 1993.

Psychology Today, "A Round-up of Rapists," November–December 1992.

RN, "History Repeats Itself When It Comes to Abuse," February 2002.

Bruce Roscoe, Jeremiah S. Strouse, and Megan P. Goodwin, "Sexual Harassment: Early Adolescents' Self-Reports of Experiences and Acceptance," *Adolescence,* Fall 1994.

Roger Rosenblatt, "The Male Response to Rape," *Time,* April 18, 1983.

Richard J. Sagall, "Sex Abuse and Teen Pregnancy," *Pediatrics for Parents,* June 1988.

Peggy R. Sanday, "The Socio-Cultural Context of Rape," *Journal of Social Issues,* 1981.

Robin G. Sawyer, Estina E. Thompson, and Anna Marie Chicorelli, "Rape Myth Acceptance Among Intercollegiate Student Athletes: A Preliminary Examination," *American Journal of Health Studies,* Winter 2002.

Stephen A. Schmidt, "To Speak of Rape: A Father's Experience," *Christian Century,* January 6, 1993.

Scholastic Choices, "Dating Danger," November–December 2001.

Lydia A. Shrier et al., "Gender Differences in Risk Behaviors Associated with Forced or Pressured Sex," *Archives of Pediatrics and Adolescent Medicine,* January 1998.

Suzanne Smalley, "'The Perfect Crime': GHB Is Colorless, Odorless, Leaves the Body Within Hours—and Is Fueling a Growing Number of Rapes," *Newsweek,* February 3, 2003.

Paige Hall Smith, Jacquelyn W. White, and Lindsay J. Holland, "A Longitudinal Perspective on Dating Violence Among Adolescent and College-Age Women," *American Journal of Public Health,* July 2003.

Jill Smolowe, "Sex with a Scoreboard," *Time,* April 5, 1993.

Kaaren Sorensen, "Dating Violence: Teens in Abusive Relationships," *Scholastic Choices,* March 2002.

Michelle Stacey, "Bad Boys," *Seventeen,* November 1993.

Kelly Starling, "Black Women and Rape: The Shocking Secret No One Talks About," *Ebony,* November 1998.

Laura Strickland, "Healing in Helping: A Rape-Victim's Story of Recovery," *Psychology Today,* March–April 2002.

Scott Suttell, "Care of Rape Victims Takes SANE Approach," *Crain's Cleveland Business,* October 6, 1997.

Mimi Swartz, "Brenham's Paradise Lost," *Texas Monthly,* February 1997.

Kimberly Coniff Taber, "I Was at a Party," *CosmoGirl!* June 2002.

Teen Magazine, "On the Defense," March 1994.

———, "Rape: The Scary Reality," November 1994.

Susan K. Telljohann et al., "High School Students' Perceptions on Nonconsensual Sexual Activity," *Journal of School Health,* March 1995.

Time, "Irresponsible Acts," March 29, 1993.

Craig Tomashoff, "Fatal Attractions: Teens Across America Are Hoping to Find Love on the Internet, but Too Many of Them Are Falling Prey to an Online World of Adult Lust and Cruel Deception. Here Are Two Girls' Stories," *Teen People,* August 1, 2002.

Anastasia Toufexis, "Our Violent Kids: A Rise in Brutal Crimes by the Young Shakes the Soul of Society," *Time,* June 12, 1989.

———, "Sex and the Sporting Life: Do Athletic Teams Unwittingly Promote Assaults and Rapes?" *Time,* August 6, 1990.

———, "Teenagers and Sex Crimes: A New Jersey Assault Dramatizes the Rise in Offenses by Youths," *Time,* June 5, 1989.

Beth Weinhouse, "Young but Not Innocent: A Shocking Report on Kids Who Rape," *Redbook,* April 1990.

Cheryl Wetzstein, "Teen Pregnancy Rate Reaches Record Low," *Insight on the News,* July 30, 2001.

Nancy Worcester, "A More Hidden Crime: Adolescent Battered Women," *Network News,* July–August 1993.

Internet Sources
American Academy of Pediatrics, "News from the AAP: Adolescent Victims of Sexual Assault Need Special Care," June 2001. www.medem.com.

The American College of Obstetricians and Gynecologists, *Drawing the Line: A Guide to Developing Sexual Assault Prevention Programs for Middle School Students,* 2000. www.acog.org.

Jeff Benedict, "Athletes and Accusations," *New York Times,* August 5, 2003. www.nytimes.com.

Rebecca Campbell, "Mental Health Services for Rape Survivors: Current Issues in Therapeutic Practice," October 2001. www.vaw.umn.edu.

The Commonwealth Fund, "The Commonwealth Fund Survey of the Health of Adolescent Girls," November 1997. www.cmwf.org.

Maggie Fox, "Hour of TV a Day Leads to Violence, Study Says," Children Now, March 28, 2002. www.childrennow.org.

Lawrence A. Greenfeld, "Sex Offenses and Offenders: An Analysis of Data on Rape and Sexual Assault," Violence Against Women Online Resources, February 1997. www.vaw.umn.edu.

Holly Harner, "Sexual Violence and Adolescents," Violence Against Women Online Resources, May 2003. www.vaw.umn.edu.

Michael Janofsky, "Air Force Begins an Inquiry of Ex-Cadets' Rape Charges," *New York Times,* February 20, 2003. www.nytimes.com.

Michael Janofsky with Diana Jean Schemo, "Women Recount cadet Life: Forced Sex and Fear," *New York Times,* March 16, 2003. www.nytimes.com.

Dean G. Kilpatrick, "The Mental Health Impact of Rape," National Violence Against Women Prevention Research Center, 2000. www.vawprevention.org.

———, "Rape and Sexual Assault," National Violence Against Women Prevention Research Center, 2000. www.vawprevention.org.

Patti Levin, "The Trauma Response," VAWnet Library, 1989. www.vawnet.org.

Frederick Mathews, "The Invisible Boy: Revisioning the Victimization of Male Children and Teens," the National Clearinghouse on Family Violence of Health Canada, 1996. www.hc-sc.gc.ca.

Urvia McDowell and Ted G. Futris, "Teen Dating Violence: Are You Aware?" Ohio State University Extension Fact Sheet, 2001. www.ohioline.osu.edu.

Medical Letter on the CDC and FDA, "Effects of Dating Violence Studied," November 12, 2000. www.NewsRx.com.

National Center for Injury Prevention and Control, "Dating Violence Fact Sheet," 2000. www.cdc.gov.

———, "Intimate Partner Violence Fact Sheet," 2002. www.cdc.gov.

———, "Rape Fact Sheet," 2000. www.cdc.gov.

The National Council on Crime and Delinquency, with assistance from the National Center for Victims of Crime, Our Vulnerable Teenagers: Their Victimization, Its Consequences, and Directions for Prevention and Intervention, May 2002. www.ncvc.org.

National Sexual Violence Resource Center, "NSVRC's Crime Statistics Obscure a Clear Picture of Sexual Assault Says the NSVRC," June 19, 2001. www.nsvrc.org.

———, "One in Five Teenage Girls Experiences Dating Violence," 2001. www.nsvrc.org.

———, "Teen Dating Violence," 2002. www.nsvrc.org.

———, "Violence Against Women on College Campuses," 2002. www.nsvrc.org.

National Youth Violence Prevention Resource Center, "Teen Dating Violence," 2003. www.safeyouth.org.

Nemours Foundation's Center for Children's Health Media, "Date Rape: What You Should Know," 2002. www.kids health.org.

———, "I Think I Was Raped. What Should I Do?" 2002. www.kidshealth.org.

New York Times, "Pentagon Panel Will Examine Air Force Sex Assault Policies," February 17, 2003. www.nytimes.com.

The Rape, Abuse, and Incest National Network (RAINN), "RAINN Statistics," 2002. www.rainn.org.

———, "What Should I Do?" Retrieved August 9, 2003. www.rainn.org.

Cathy Schoen et al., "The Commonwealth Fund Survey of the Health of Adolescent Girls," The Commonwealth Fund, November 1997. www.cmwf.org.

———, "The Health of Adolescent Boys: Commonwealth Fund Survey Findings," The Common-wealth Fund, November 1997. www.cmwf.org.

Nan Stein, "Sexual Harassment in Schools," National Violence Against Women Prevention Research Center, 2000. www.vawprevention.org.

Jonathan C. Stillerman, "Male Survivors of Sexual Assault," Men Can Stop Rape, 2003. www.mencanstoprape.org.

U.S. Department of Justice, "Bureau of Justice Statistics Factbook, Violence by Intimates," March 1998. www.ojp.usdoj.gov.

———, "Bureau of Justice Statistics, National Crime Victimization Survey, Criminal Victimization 2001, Changes 2000–01 with Trends 1993–2001," September 2002. www.ojp. usdoj.gov.

———, "Bureau of Justice Statistics, Selected Findings, Rape and Sexual Assault: Reporting to Police and Medical Attention, 1992–2000." www.ojp.usdoj.gov.

———, "Bureau of Justice Statistics Special Report, Intimate Partner Violence," May 2000. www.ojp.usdoj.gov.

———, "Crime Data Brief, Child Rape Victims, 1992," June 1994. www.ojp.usdoj.gov.

———, "Full Report of the Prevalence, Incidence, and Consequences of Violence Against Women, Findings from the National Violence Against Women Survey," November 2000. www.ojp.usdoj.gov.

David A. Wolfe and Peter G. Jaffe, "Prevention of Domestic Violence and Sexual Assault," Violence Against Women Online Resources, January 2003. www.vaw.umn.edu.

Websites

Children, Youth, and Families Education and Research Network (CYFERnet) (www.cyfernet.org). CYFERnet is a website that draws on resources from all of the public land-grant universities in the country to provide both professionals and laypeople with research-based information on children, youth, and families. As part of the U.S. Department of Agriculture's Children, Youth, and Families at Risk Program, the site includes articles on rape, sexual assault, and abuse.

Men Overcoming Violence (MOVE) (www.menover comingviolence.org). This San Francisco, California–based nonprofit organization is dedicated to ending young and adult men's violence in their relationships. MOVE works to prevent teen dating violence and domestic violence through advocacy, training, and education. It also provides comprehensive counseling services to young men. The site includes extensive information on its youth programs.

The National Sexual Violence Resource Center (www. nsvrc.org). A project of the Pennsylvania Coalition Against Rape, this website serves as a central clearinghouse for the voluminous resources and research on sexual violence.

The National Violence Against Women Prevention Research Center (www.vawprevention.org). Sponsored by the Centers for Disease Control and Prevention, this website provides researchers, practitioners, and laypeople with up-to-date information related to violence against women and its prevention. The site includes a "For Survivors" section with resources for victims.

The National Youth Violence Prevention Resource Center (www.safeyouth.org). The National Youth Violence Prevention Resource Center is a central source of information on violence committed by and against children and teens. The website is a collaborative effort of the Centers for Disease Control and Prevention and other federal agencies. It provides up-to-date research on crimes that affect young people.

Promote Truth Website (www.promotetruth.org). Created by the Rape Recovery Team at the Women's Center of Jacksonville in Florida, this website offers online support and information for teens about sexual violence.

VAWnet Library (www.vawnet.org). A joint project of the Pennsylvania Coalition Against Domestic Violence and the National Resource Center on Domestic Violence, this website contains extensive information on domestic violence, sexual assault, and other violence in the lives of women and children.

Violence Against Women Online Resources (www.vaw. umn.edu). This site is a joint project of the Office on Violence Against Women and the Minnesota Center Against Violence and Abuse at the University of Minnesota. The site has an extensive document library on all aspects of violence against women, including rape.

Index

abuse
  in dating relationships,
    14–15, 32–33
  impact of childhood sexual,
    34
acquaintance rape, 13
  by friends and casual
    acquaintances, 15
  impact of, 47
  Internet and, 15–16
  rape myths and, 24
Air Force Academy,
  77–78
alcohol use, 26, 44
American Academy of
  Pediatrics, 67
American College of
  Obstetricians and
  Gynecologists, 71, 77
American Medical
  Association, 67
athletes, 41–42

Bosnian war, 8
boyfriends, 48–49
boys. *See* males

causes
  disrespect toward women,
    21, 21–22, 23

gender-role
  stereotypes/socialization,
    29–30
less parental support, 33
media violence, 23–24
sexuality messages and
  pressures on girls, 30–32
societal attitudes, 21
victims' dress, 28
childhood sexual abuse,
  34–36
college fraternities, 41–42
counselors, 63–64, 74
Crime Victims Research and
  Treatment Center, 10

date rape, 13–15
Date-Rape Drug Prohibition
  Act (2000), 66
date-rape drugs, 45–46
Department of Justice, 10
disabled teens, 43
DNA technology, 68
dress, rape myths on, 28
drug use, 44

family
  impact of rape on, 49–50
  incest in, 18
  reaction to rape of family
    member, 48

sexual abuse within, 34–36
support from, 60–63
traditional roles within,
  36–38
see also parents
fraternities, 41
friends
  date rape by, 15
  reaction of to rape of
    friend, 48–50
  support from, 60–63
  see also peers

gang rape, 19–20
  macho expectations and, 30
  peer pressure and, 42
gays and lesbians, 14–15
gender inequalities, 36–38,
  81
gender-role
  stereotypes/socialization,
  29–30
GHB (date-rape drug), 45
girls
  conflicting sexuality mes-
    sages and pressures on,
    30–32
  search for father figure by,
    39
  socialization and stereotypes
    of, 29–30
Gone with the Wind (film),
  27

health-care providers, 67–69
homosexuality
  gang rape and, 20

see also gays and lesbians
hospitals, 59–60

incest, 18
Internet, the, 15–16
intervention. *See* rape
  prevention

Kennedy, Michael, 16
Ketamine, 45

laws, statury-rape, 16
legal system, 50–51
Levy, Barrie, 14

males
  incest and, 18
  macho expectations of, 30
  making prevention programs
    friendly toward, 74–76
  as rape victims, 10, 18
  denial by, 55
  father absence/neglect and,
    39
  support from family/friends
    for, 61
  socialization and stereotypes
    of, 29–30
Massachusetts Youth Risk
  Behavior Survey, 14
media
  disrespect towards women
    in, 23
  parental role and, 80
  rape myths and, 27
  rape prevention and, 81
  violent imagery in, 23–24

Men Can Stop Rape, 75
Men Overcoming Violence (MOVE), 75–76

National Center for Victims of Crime, 78
National Council on Crime and Delinquency, 18, 36, 78
National Crime Victimization Survey, 10
National Victim Center, 10
National Violence Against Women Survey, 10

Our Vulnerable Teenagers (National Council on Crime and Delinquency), 36

parents
  father absence/neglect and, 39–40
  less guidance and supervision by, 33
  rape prevention and, 78–80
peers
  influence of, 40–42
  pressure by, 19, 29–30
physical abuse, 14
physical trauma, 58
physicians, 67–68
Pipher , Mary, 31–32, 35–36
police, the, 60
pornography, 23
posttraumatic stress disorder, 51

rape, 12

history of, 8
minimizing seriousness of, 26–27
prevalence of, 9
romanticizing, 27
Rape, Abuse and Incest National Network (RAINN), 9
rape crisis centers, 57
rape myths
  acquaintance rape and, 24, 47
  blaming victims and, 24–25
  drinking and, 26
  family and friends influenced by, 48–49
  romanticize rape, 27
rape prevention
  changing school and community culture and, 77–78
  gender inequality and, 81
  health-care provider screening and, 67–69
  parental role in, 78–80
  programs for
  community member involvement in, 72–74
  content of, 70–71
  effectiveness of, 71–72
  male-friendly, 74–76
  redesigning, 69–70
  teen involvement in, 72
  victim disclosure in, 74
rape trauma syndrome, 51–53
rape victims. *See* victims

rapists
  adult, 16–17
  attitudes of, 38–39
  childhood abuse and, 36
  legal action against, 65–66
recovery
  family/friend support and,
    60–63
  immediate responses after
    rape for, 57–58
  improvement in treatments
    and, 58–60
  legal action against rapists
    and, 65–66
  medical assistance and, 58
  self-care activities and, 65
  support groups and, 64–65
  therapy, 63–64
risk factors
  disabilities, 43
  family background, 34–40
  lack of control over
    circumstances, 46
  low self-esteem, 42–43
  peers, 40–42
  situational, 43–46
Rohypnol, 44–45
runaways, 36

Safe Harbor program, 74
schools
  changing culture in, 77–78
  prevention programs in, 70,
    72–74
  sexual harassment in, 32
secondary victimization,
  48–49

self-esteem, 42–43
sexual abuse, 34–36
sexual assault, 9
  see also rape; teen rape
Sexual Assault Nurse
  Examiners (SANEs),
  59–60
sexual harassment, 32
sexually transmitted
  diseases, 58
sexual promiscuity, 56
Spur Posse gang, 26–27, 43
statutory rape, 16–17
stranger rape, 18–19
street gangs, 42
substance abuse, 44

teen pregnancy, 34–35
teen rape
  impact of, 47
  prevalence of, 10
  revictimization and, 10
Teen Victim Project, 78
television, 23, 24
therapy, 63–64
treatment. *See* recovery
trials, rape, 50–51

victims
  age of, at time of first rape,
    11
  avoidance by, 53–54
  blaming, 24–25, 28
  denial by, 54–55
  disabled, 43
  drugged, 44–46
  false accusations by, 27

harassment of, by rapists' supporters, 50
influence of family and friend reactions on, 49–50
legal system's treatment of, 50–51
rape trauma syndrome of, 51–53
reporting rape, 11–12, 48
revictimization of, 56
self-destructive behavior by, 55–56
silence of, 47–48
see also males, as rape victims; recovery
video games, 24
violence, in the media, 23–24

Wellesley College Center for Research on Women, 72

Youth Relationship Project, 76

Picture Credits

Cover: © Creasource/Series/Picture Quest
© Mark C. Burnett/Photo Researchers, Inc., 37
© Custom Medical Stock Photo, 59, 73
© Getty Images, 25, 26, 35, 61
© David M. Grossman/Photo Researchers, Inc., 40
© John Henley/CORBIS, 49, 79
© 2002 Marilyn Humphries, 76
© Richard Hutchings/Photo Researchers, Inc., 20
© Catherine Karnow/Woodfin Camp and Associates, 68
© Rob Lewine/CORBIS, 52
© Damien Lovegrove/Science Photo Library, 55
© LWA-Stephen Welstead/CORBIS, 62
© Cheryl Maeder/CORBIS, 31
© Lawrence Manning/CORBIS, 13, 28, 54
© Royalty-Free/CORBIS, 65
© Chuck Savage/CORBIS, 45
© Ariel Skelley/CORBIS, 41
© 2002 Jim West, 17
© 2003 Jim West, 80
© Stefan Zaklin/Reuters/Landov, 22

About the Author

Lynn Slaughter has written more than one hundred magazine articles about teenagers, parenting, and family relationships. She holds BA and MA degrees in sociology from Smith College and the University of Arizona, respectively, and an MA in dance education from the University of Michigan. The former chair of the dance department at the Youth Performing Arts School, she currently divides her time between writing and counseling teenagers at Kentucky's Governor's School for the Arts. She lives in Louisville, Kentucky with her family.